THE BEST OF STOVELINE

D1593245

𝕿𝖍𝖊 𝕾𝖕𝖊𝖈𝖙𝖆𝖙𝖔𝖗

Published by
The Spectator
44 Frid Street,
Hamilton, Ont. L8N 3G3

Production by
North Shore Publishing
Burlington, Ont.

Recipes - Norma Bidwell
Publication co-ordinator - Gary Evans
Cover design - Helen Witkowski

Canadian Cataloguing in Publication Data

The Best of Stoveline
Bidwell, Norma

ISBN 0-9698460-2-9

Printed and bound in Canada
First printing - November, 1994

Introduction

One of the most heart-warming letters I ever received from a Stoveline reader came from a mother of two teenaged sons who wrote: "It has taken me 16 years to write this letter and a book full of newspaper clippings. You're my adopted cooking Mom. I feel very warm towards you although we've never met. Your smile, frequent mention of your family (I have two sons 17 and 20) and your helpful, caring ways. May God bless you and give you many more productive years."

Nearly 15 years ago when I retired as food editor of The Spectator, I began writing Stoveline, a weekly column where readers could have their food queries answered. From the mass of each week's mail, several letters are chosen to make up my Stoveline column. The rest of the mail I answer personally.

Some of the mail is a nostalgic yearning for dishes readers remember from childhood. Crisp cookies, zesty soups, creamy puddings, stick-to-the-ribs stews, towering layer cakes wicked with home-cooked icings their mothers or grandmothers used to make.

Sadly, many of these delectable, mouth-watering dishes were not from written-down recipes, but from cooking lore passed down from one generation to the next through hands-on experience.

Readers write letters like, "My mother used to make the most wonderful thing for us when we were small. My brother and I only remember it had milk and sugar and eggs and smelled so good while it was cooking. Please send me the recipe because I want to make it for my grandchildren." This calls for a phone chat to discover whether it was a pudding, cake, pie or even a coffee cake.

Often, I find I have a similar recipe in my own hand-written recipe books. When I am completely stumped, a plea goes out through Stoveline and a flood of mail brings different readers' versions of the sought recipe. To all readers who have taken the time and trouble over the years to send in their own recipes, my most heartfelt thanks. Because of the volume of mail, it is not possible to thank each one personally.

Many of the requests are for dishes enjoyed in hotels or restaurants, both in this country and abroad, or from bakeries long out of existence. Unless they are for classical dishes like Sasher Torte or Beef Wellington, for which recipes are widely available, these requests are, of course, impossible to answer.

It is especially gratifying to have letters from children like one that read, "Do you answer kids' questions or from only moms and dads? I want to make muffins all by myself but I need help. My mom works and is too busy to teach me how."

Or, from men who are single fathers, painstakingly learning their way around the kitchen, wanting nutritious recipes to make for the children they are raising.

This cookbook is a small sampling of the many readers' letters and my answers that have appeared in my Stoveline columns over the years. Most of the recipes are cook-friendly, easy to do and use ingredients you likely have on hand. Few readers ask for gourmet recipes, calorie-wise, or low in fat, salt or sugar recipes. The cookbook market abounds with these volumes. This book is like a lost and found column of treasured mom-type ways of turning out those wonderful, dearly remembered childhood treats.

Happy memories and tastings,

Norma

Contents

Dedication

For my dear husband, Fred, for his help and
encouragement all along the way.

Soups

Blender Hamburger Soup   *Serves 10-12*

Dear Norma/
I have a blender but no food processor. All the recipes I see lately seem to be for the processor. I like to make my own soup and would like a recipe for a meat soup utilizing my blender.

Answer/
You can make a great hamburger-vegetable soup in no time using your blender. This is a big recipe and you could freeze half for future use.

3 1/2 cups canned tomatoes	4 large sprigs parsley
2 (10-oz.) cans condensed consommé	10 black peppercorns
	1 1/2 lbs. medium ground beef
2 cups water	3 tbsp. salad oil
1 medium onion, peeled and quartered	1 bay leaf
	2 tsp. salt
4 medium carrots, cut into chunks	1/4 tsp. pepper
	1/2 tsp. sugar
4 celery tops	Few drops Tabasco

Combine tomatoes, consommé, water, onion, carrots, celery tops, parsley and peppercorns in large saucepan; simmer, covered, for 25 minutes. Cool. Put half of mixture in blender container and run on high for one minute or until vegetables are pureed. Empty into large sauce pan. Repeat process with remaining soup. Meanwhile, brown meat in oil, breaking it apart as it cooks. Add to soup with remaining seasonings; cover and simmer 20 minutes.

Best Ever Vegetable Beef Soup   *Serves 8*

Dear Norma/
Would you have a good recipe for vegetable-beef soup that doesn't take hours of cooking? Our Saturday night supper for our family of six is always a hearty soup and homemade bread.

Answer/
Start with ground beef and it will cut down the cooking time to less than an hour. You'll like the rich, robust flavor of this soup. If you have a freezer, double the batch and freeze half. It's like money in the bank to have a meal of good soup in the freezer.

1 lb. ground beef	1/2 cup pasta stars or elbow
2 cups chopped onion	macaroni
1 cup chopped celery	2 bay leaves
1 cup thinly-sliced carrots	2 tsp. each of chili powder and
6 cups water	basil
3 tbsp. beef bouillon powder	1 tsp. salt
28-oz. can tomatoes,	1/8 tsp. pepper
undrained, cut up	2 (14-oz.) cans kitchen-sliced
7 1/2-oz. can tomato sauce	cut green beans, drained

In large heavy saucepan, brown ground beef; drain fat. Add onion, celery and carrots and stir and cook for five minutes. Add remaining ingredients, except green beans, and bring to a boil. Reduce heat. Cover and simmer 40 minutes. Stir in green beans and cook until heated through or until vegetables and pasta are tender. Discard bay leaves and serve hot.

Meatball Soup

Dear Norma/

Recently I was visiting my brother in Washington and he asked if I remembered our mother's meatball soup. It was a hearty vegetable soup with meatballs dropped in near the last. Do you have a recipe along these lines?

Answer/

One of my favorite cookbooks was published a few years ago by St. Elizabeth's Anglican Church in Burlington and this is the first recipe in the book.

6 cups beef stock (or use six beef bouillon cubes and six cups boiling water)
1/2 cup diced carrots
1/2 cup thinly-sliced green onions
1/2 cup finely-chopped celery
1/2 cup diced turnip
12 oz. can whole kernel corn
28-oz. can tomatoes

1/4 tsp. sweet leaf basil
Salt and pepper to taste
2 slices day-old bread
1 lb. ground beef
1 egg, slightly beaten
Pinch thyme
1 1/2 tsp. salt
1/8 tsp. pepper
2 tbsp. butter
Grated Parmesan cheese

Combine beef stock, vegetables and sweet basil in large saucepan; bring to boil; turn down heat and simmer 15 minutes. Taste and add salt and pepper to taste.

To make meatballs, moisten bread with cold water and squeeze out all excess water and break bread into small pieces. Mix with meat, egg, thyme, salt and pepper and form into small balls. Heat butter in large skillet and add meatballs. Brown lightly on all sides. Lift as they brown and add to soup. Simmer soup, covered, 30 minutes more, when all meatballs have been added. Ladle into soup bowls and pass Parmesan cheese to sprinkle, if desired.

Tomato-Beef Soup

Dear Norma/

I'm not one of those cooks who pride themselves on not using packaged or canned foods. I love the convenience of combining them into "homemade" dishes. I would like an easy recipe (using canned soup if possible) for a meal-in-a-dish.

Answer/

Everything in this soup is canned or packaged except the water! But when you put it all together, you can pass it off as homemade without raising anyone's eyebrows.

1 to 1 1/2 lbs. lean ground beef
1 package (2 envelopes) Lipton tomato-vegetable soup mix
3 cans condensed cream of tomato soup
1/2 cup uncooked small macaroni
1 cup sliced or diced leftover vegetables (or fresh or frozen)
10 soup cans water

Brown meat in large kettle (one that doesn't stick or burn). Add all other ingredients; stir, bring to boil and then simmer for 15 minutes or until macaroni is cooked. Keeps well in refrigerator. Makes a huge pot of soup. Half could be frozen.

Broccoli Soup
Serves 4 to 6

Dear Norma/

I would like your recipe for creamy broccoli soup - the one with some curry powder.

Answer/

You will need a food processor for this soup and it can be made with or without cream.

1 bunch broccoli, washed
3 tbsp. butter
1 onion, chopped
3 tbsp. flour
3 tbsp. curry powder (or to taste)
4 to 6 cups chicken stock
Salt and pepper to taste
Cream (optional)

If you use cream, reduce the amount of chicken stock. Cut off coarse stems and peel broccoli. Steam until tender. In saucepan, melt butter and gently sauté onion and curry powder. Stir in flour and cook, stirring, for one minute. Add hot stock and stir until boiling. Puree broccoli in blender or food processor and add to hot stock. Add seasoning to taste. Cream can be added; taste and correct seasonings. Serve hot or cold.

Cream of Cauliflower Soup   *Serves 3-4*

Dear Norma/

I am cooking for two and we both love cauliflower, but a head lasts so long that I usually have to throw some out. Could you give me a recipe for cream of cauliflower soup that would use half a head of cauliflower?

Answer/

Here it is and because it has cheese added it is hearty enough for a luncheon or supper meal. Freeze half if you like.

1/2 medium head cauliflower, chopped
2 tbsp. butter or margarine
2 tbsp. chopped onion
2 tbsp. flour
1 1/2 cups chicken broth
1 cup milk
1/2 tsp. Worcestershire sauce
Cauliflower and cooking water
1/2 cup shredded Cheddar cheese
Sprinkle of herbs

Cook cauliflower in boiling, salted water until soft. Keep cooking water. Sauté in a large saucepan, until yellow, the onion and butter or margarine. Blend in the flour. Add the chicken broth, milk, Worcestershire sauce, cauliflower and cooking water. Cook until the mixture thickens slightly. Add the cheese and stir to melt the cheese. Serve sprinkled with herbs. Or, you can whirl the soup in a blender or processor if you prefer a smooth soup. For cream of zucchini soup, use 2 or 3 medium zucchini instead of cauliflower.

Pot of Bean Soup
Serves 6

Dear Norma/
The long slow simmering of a pot of homemade soup leaves me cold. I want to grab my can opener and whip up something "homemade" in a hurry. Have you any recipes for a quick soup for chilly fall days?

Answer/
Here is a trio of quickies you couldn't make without your can opener.

2 (28-oz.) cans beans with pork   **2 tbsp. barbecue sauce**
1 (28-oz.) can tomatoes

Put all the ingredients in a big pot. Cook together over low heat for a few minutes. Get out the crackers and serve.

Hot Tomato Bouillon
Serves 4 to 5

14-oz. can beef broth	**Few drops Worcestershire**
12-oz. can tomato juice	**sauce**
	Few drops Tabasco sauce

Bring to a boil and simmer one minute. Garnish in soup bowls with very thin slices of lemon.

Wonderful Canned Soup

1 large can chunky	**12 rings small salami or**
beef-vegetable soup	**similar sausage**
10-oz. can consommé	**Butter**
1 can ravioli	**Water**
1 1/2 cups finely-shredded	
cabbage	

Sauté cabbage and salami in butter. Add water to soups as per directions. Add cabbage, salami and ravioli. Simmer a few minutes and serve.

Cabbage Soup

Dear Norma/

When the colder weather comes, I use a lot of hearty supper dishes for my family. They love homemade soup and I wonder if you have one using ground beef.

Answer/

When the wind howls and the snow is blowing against the kitchen window, I always think it is cabbage soup time. This is a whole meal in a bowl.

1 lb. ground beef	1/2 tsp. paprika
1 onion	1 quart stewed tomatoes
1/2 cup celery, chopped	2 small cans tomato paste
1/2 cup green pepper, chopped	4 cups hot water
Sauté first four ingredients.	2 beef bouillon cubes
Add:	3 tbsp. chopped parsley
2 tsp. salt	2 cups diced raw potato
2 tbsp. sugar	1 cup diced raw carrots
1/4 tsp. pepper	

Simmer for one hour and then add 1/2 cup shredded cabbage. Cook for 15 minutes more and serve. Makes a big pot of hearty soup.

Brown Potato Soup

Serves 8

Dear Norma/

Having found so many family favorites in your columns over the years, I am delighted to respond to another reader's request for her mother's soup made with browned flour. This is truly delicious, both satisfying and delicate. Hope it is what your reader had in mind.

Answer/

Many readers must have enjoyed "brown soup" in their growing-up years. Thanks to everyone who sent in their favorite version of this inexpensive family soup.

4 cups peeled, diced potatoes	1/2 tsp. black pepper
1/2 cup diced celery	2 cups light cream
1 large cooking onion, thinly	3 cups milk
sliced	2 tbsp. butter
2 1/2 cups boiling water	1/2 cup all-purpose flour
1 1/2 tsp. salt	

Combine vegetables, water, salt and pepper in large saucepan and cook, covered, until vegetables are just tender. Add cream and milk and bring back to boiling point, then turn heat low. Melt butter in small, heavy skillet; add flour off heat. Return to heat and cook and stir until roux (flour and butter mixture) is rich brown. Add some vegetable liquid to brown roux, stirring until smoothly blended and add this mixture to saucepan, stirring constantly. Cover and simmer five minutes, lifting cover to stir several times. Serve very hot.

Blueberry Soup

Dear Norma/

I have a china soup tureen that belonged to my grandmother and I would like to be able to use it in the summer as well as in the cold months. Could you give me some recipes for cold soups?

Answer/

Chilled soups are an absolute delight in the dog days of summer. Don't forget to chill both the tureen and soup bowls. You might even use some clear glass bowls for these chilly soups.

1 1/2 cups blueberries, washed 2 tbsp. cornstarch
1 qt. water   3 tbsp. water
1/4 cup sugar

Place water and blueberries in pot. Simmer until very soft. Strain berries through sieve and return to saucepan. Mix cornstarch and three tablespoons water, add to soup and cook, stirring until thickened. Stir, adding sugar. Simmer three minutes. Chill and serve.

Cucumber-Buttermilk Soup

2 (10-oz.) cans mushroom soup   1/2 cup minced celery
2 cups buttermilk   2 tbsp. minced green onions
1 cup minced, seeded cucumbers

Mix all together thoroughly and chill.

Salads

Salad Nicoise
Serves 4

Dear Norma/

Ever since I tasted Salad Nicoise in a fine hotel in California, I have wanted to make one for a summer party at home. My recipe books don't have it and I would love to have a recipe to serve 12 for lunch.

Answer/

This French provincial classic recipe is named after Nice, where it is believed to have originated. It's a complete meal in itself. Just add some hot rolls and perhaps an ice cream pie with a fresh fruit topping for dessert.

2 lettuce hearts	1 hard-boiled egg, cut into
2 cans solid white tuna	wedges
10 or so pitted black olives	1/2 cup olive oil
1 onion, cut into rings	4 tbsp. white wine vinegar
2 tomatoes, cut into wedges	1/4 tsp. dried tarragon
1/4 lb. string beans, cooked	1/4 tsp. dried dill
1 green pepper, cut into strips	Salt and pepper to taste
	1 clove garlic, crushed

Wash and dry lettuce and tear into bite-sized pieces. Line nice platter with lettuce. Mound tuna in centre and garnish platter attractively with olives, onion rings, tomatoes, beans, pepper strips and hard-boiled egg. Make vinaigrette dressing by combining rest of ingredients in screw-top jar and shake well to combine thoroughly. Pour dressing over salad just before serving.

This recipe serves four and can be adapted to serve 12 by tripling each ingredient.

Baked Corn Beef Salad

Dear Norma/
I have several cans of corned beef in my cupboard and would like to use some of it in a salad or casserole.

Answer/
While this is called a salad, likely because of the mayonnaise in it, it is baked and served hot. So it is either a hot salad or a casserole.

2 (12 oz.) cans corned beef, flaked (remove fat)	1/4 cup chopped onion
1 cup chopped celery	1 tbsp. prepared mustard
1/2 cup chopped olives or pickle relish	Dash of black pepper
	3/4 cup mayonnaise
2 hard-cooked eggs	1 cup potato chips, crushed (optional)

Combine all ingredients except potato chips and put into buttered casserole or loaf pan. Top with potato chips if desired. Bake for 20 minutes in 400F oven.

Sauerkraut Salad

Dear Norma/
I bought a jar of sauerkraut salad at a church bake sale and it is the greatest relish I've ever tasted. I know you can't have this exact recipe but would you have anything similar?

Answer/
I've had this recipe for donkey's years and I never call it Saurerkraut salad because so many people think they don't like sauerkraut. But everyone loves this and it keeps in a covered jar in the fridge for a long time.

1 large tin sauerkraut, drained	1 cup chopped carrots
	Bring to a boil:
1 cup chopped onion	1/2 cup vinegar
1 cup chopped celery	1/2 cup salad oil
1 cup chopped green pepper	1 1/2 cups sugar

Pour boiling sauce over prepared vegetables. Marinate and chill overnight before using. Keep in covered jar in refrigerator.

Hot Mushroom Salad   *Serves 4*

Dear Norma/
  Do you happen to have a recipe in your files for a hot mushroom salad? I tasted it at a friend's house and loved it but didn't like to ask for the recipe.

Answer/
  There are many ways of making a hot mushroom salad so this one may not resemble the one you remember.

1/2 lb. mushrooms	1 1/2 tbsp. soy sauce
1 green pepper, cut in thin strips	1 1/2 tbsp. teriyaki sauce
	Lettuce
1 small onion, thinly sliced	3 slices bacon, cooked until crisp and crumbled
1 tbsp. melted butter or margarine	

  Combine all ingredients except lettuce and bacon in a skillet or wok. Cook, stirring frequently just until mushrooms and onion are tender. Have lettuce arranged on four salad plates; spoon hot mixture onto lettuce, sprinkle with bacon and serve at once.

Pasta Shells Creamy Salad   *Serves 8*

Dear Norma/
My family loves macaroni salad and I am wondering if you have a recipe for a summer salad using those tiny pasta shells? With cheese, if possible. There are eight of us.

Answer/
I always think it is easier to cook for a crowd than for two or three so here is a recipe tailored to your big family. You could use hot dog mustard, but Dijon is much nicer.

2 cups (raw) tiny pasta shells, cooked and well drained	**1/4 cup chopped celery**
	1/4 cup shredded carrot
1/2 cup creamy Italian dressing	**2 cups shredded old cheddar cheese (8 oz.)**
1/4 cup chopped onion (try red onion for a change)	**1/2 cup mayonnaise or salad dressing**
1/4 cup chopped green pepper	**1 tsp. prepared mustard**
1/4 cup chopped pimiento	

In large bowl, combine hot pasta and Italian salad dressing; mix well. Add onion, green pepper, pimiento, celery and carrot. Toss to mix well. Chill. Toss cheese with chilled pasta mixture. In small bowl, mix mayonnaise and mustard. Fold into pasta mixture. Refrigerate, covered, until serving time.

Note: Any pasta salad improves with time so make well ahead of serving.

Fresh Spinach Salad

Dear Norma/
My husband just loves the spinach salad he gets in a Burlington restaurant where they serve it with chicken wings. I know you can't duplicate this commercial recipe but do you have one that might be close?

Answer/
There are dozens of ways of making a spinach salad but here is one that my own family asks for time and again. It is best made with fresh bunch spinach rather than the cello-pack.

1 garlic clove, halved
2 tbsp. red wine vinegar
1 tsp. sugar
1 tsp. salt
1 tsp. dry mustard
1/2 tsp. freshly ground pepper
6 tbsp. salad oil
8 cups crisp, young spinach,
　hard stems removed
　(2 to 2 1/2 lbs.)
3 hard-cooked eggs, grated

8 slices side bacon, cooked
　until crisp and crumbled
　(bacon bits are not an
　acceptable substitute)
3 green onions, chopped finely
2 cups garlic croutons
Lots of fresh mushrooms, cut
　T-shaped
Fresh cauliflower, sliced,
　T-shaped (optional)

Beat first seven ingredients and refrigerate. Prepare the remaining ingredients. Add dressing just before serving, after removing garlic.

Erie Beach Hotel Bean Salad

Dear Norma/
    My dad and I have a guys' day out every year and go for a big feed of perch at that hotel in Port Dover. My mom said somebody told her you have the recipees for their horseradish salad and bean salad and if I can get them from you, she will make some at home.
    I am 12 years old and hope I spelled everything okay. Please answer.

Answer/
    I answer all my reader mail to Stoveline either through the column or personally. You did fine in spelling except for recipe which has only one "e".

2 (19-oz.) tins green beans, drained
2 (19-oz.) tins yellow beans, drained
19-oz. tin chick peas, drained
15-oz. tin red kidney beans, washed and drained
2 medium onions, cut into rings

1 cup cauliflower, diced
1 cup baby carrots, cooked
Dressing:
1 cup white sugar
1 cup vinegar
1/2 cup salad oil
1 1/2 tsp. salt
1 1/2 tsp. pepper

    Put dressing ingredients in jar and shake well. Pour over well-drained vegetables. Refrigerate for a day before using.

Erie Beach Hotel Horseradish Salad

1 package lemon jelly powder
1 1/2 cups boiling water
1/2 cup whipping cream, whipped stiff

1/2 cup mayonnaise
4 tbsp. well-drained horseradish
Another package jelly powder

    Dissolve jelly powder in boiling water. Cool. When jelly becomes syrupy add whipped cream, mayonnaise and horse-radish. Blend thoroughly. Rinse eight-inch square cake pan in cold water and put jelly mixture in, spreading evenly. Let set. In meantime, make up one package lemon or pineapple jelly powder using one cup boiling water to dissolve and one cup cold water. When first jelly mixture is well set, pour lemon or pineapple mixture over and refrigerate until set. Cut in squares to serve.

Curried Turkey Salad   *Serves 6 to 8*

Dear Norma/

Before Christmas, I like to collect a file of ways to deal with leftover turkey and meals to serve between Christmas and New Year's Day. Do you have a good turkey salad recipe?

Answer/

What a good idea! No searching through piles of recipes to locate what you want at a specific time. Try this turkey salad recipe if you like a whiff of curry.

1/2 cup mayonnaise
1/2 cup plain yogurt
1/4 cup dairy sour cream
2 tbsp. lemon juice
2 tsp. curry powder
1 1/2 tsp. onion salt
4 cups diced, cooked turkey

1/2 cup chopped celery
1 cup diced fresh pineapple or
   diced apple
1 head Boston lettuce, washed
   and dried
1 bunch watercress, washed
   and dried

In a large bowl, mix together all ingredients except lettuce and watercress. Arrange these greens in large serving bowl or on individual places, and place a mound of the turkey salad in the centre of each.

Frozen Fruit Salad *Serves 8 to 10*

Dear Norma/
When I was young, a friend would make a salad in a loaf pan. This was frozen, then sliced and served on a lettuce leaf. The ingredients included fruit cocktail, cream cheese and nuts. We have been unable to locate this recipe, but I'm sure you can come up with it.

Answer/
This won't be your exact recipe, but here is one I have made for years. You could substitute walnuts for the pecans and fruit salad for the pineapple. It needs to be only partially frozen. Women like it; men are iffy about it, so save it for bridge club.

2 (3-oz.) packages plain cream cheese	1/2 cup coarsely chopped, toasted pecans
1 cup Miracle Whip salad dressing	1 can (2 1/2 cups) crushed pineapple, well drained
1 cup whipping cream, whipped	24 large size marshmallows, cut in thirds (don't substitute miniature marshmallows)
1/2 cup each red and green maraschino cherries, quartered	

Combine room temperature cream cheese and salad dressing and blend until smooth. Fold in whipped cream, fruit, nuts and marshmallows. Spoon into one-quart loaf pan or refrigerator tray, cover with foil and put in freezer until firm. Move to refrigerator 30 minutes before serving.

Serve in semi-frozen state on lettuce leaf with small gherkin pickles, tiny celery curls and small, warmed Parker House rolls.

Ambrosia Salad

Serves 4

Dear Norma/

I would like a recipe for a fancy fruit salad to serve in lettuce cups when I have "the girls" in for lunch. These aren't calorie-counters so make it nice and rich.

Answer/

This is strictly for the girls. I don't think many men would fancy it.

3 tart apples, peeled, cored
  and diced
2 tbsp. lemon juice
1/2 cup diced celery
1 cup well-drained pineapple
  tidbits
1/2 cup chopped toasted
  walnuts or pecans

1 cup seeded grapes
  (or seedless)
1/2 cup quartered or
  miniature marshmallows
1/4 cup mayonnaise
1 cup whipped cream

Dice apples into lemon juice to prevent discoloring. Drain. Combine with next five ingredients, then fold in mayonnaise blended with whipped cream. Serve in lettuce cups with hot rolls or croissants.

Vegetables

Not-the-same-old Cabbage — *Serves 6 to 8*

Dear Norma/

Our family enjoys cooked cabbage and sometimes when vegetables are high priced during the winter months we have it often. I get bored with it. Would you have a way of dressing it up a little. Nothing too complicated, please.

Answer/

You don't say how large your family is but this tasty cabbage dish will serve eight and I will guarantee it isn't boring.

4 tbsp. butter	1 head cabbage (2 lb.),
1 large Bermuda or Spanish	quartered and cut into
onion, chopped fine	thin slices
2 large green tart apples,	1/3 cup light brown sugar
peeled, quartered and cut	1/2 cup vinegar
into thin slices, or chopped	Salt and pepper to taste
1 cup water	

Melt butter in heavy four-quart pot (I use the pot of my pressure cooker). Add onion and sauté over medium heat until transparent, stirring occasionally. Add apples, cabbage and water. Cook, covered, over low heat for one hour, stirring occasionally. Add sugar and vinegar, combine and simmer five to 10 minutes. Add salt and pepper to taste.

Red Cabbage and Apples   *Serves 6 to 8*

Dear Norma/
  I see red cabbage in the supermarket and would buy it if I knew what to do with it. I don't like it shredded in salad.

Answer/
  Red cabbage can be served right from the pot, but I always think a half hour in the oven improves it.

3-lb. red cabbage	**2 tbsp. bacon fat (don't**
2 green apples, peeled, cored	**substitute anything else)**
and chopped	**1 tsp. salt**
1 onion, chopped finely	**Freshly-ground black pepper**
1/4 cup white sugar	**1/2 cup boiling water**
1/4 cup red wine vinegar	

  Shred cabbage, discarding core. Put in heavy saucepan with apples, onion, sugar, vinegar, bacon fat, salt and pepper. Stir until mixed. Add half cup boiling water, bring to a boil and reduce heat. Cover and simmer 45 minutes, stirring occasionally. Transfer to greased casserole and bake at 350F for 30 minutes, covered.

Perfect Fried Onions

Dear Norma/
  I hope you won't think this is a silly request but I don't have any luck frying onions. Mine turn out greasy and often burnt. I would like the rings to stay whole if possible.

Answer/
  No kitchen cry for help is silly! If you have a well-seasoned cast-iron frying pan, use it for this way of making perfect fried onions to go with liver or steak.

3 large cooking onions	**3 tbsp butter (don't substitute)**
2 tbsp. cold water	**Salt, pepper and sage**

  Slice the onion about 3/4-inch thick and peel slices. Put the cold water, butter and then onions in a frying pan. Sprinkle with salt, pepper and sage. Cook, over medium heat, covered, for the first five minutes then uncover and cook until golden brown over a slightly higher heat. Turn with a broad spatula, but not too often, to keep onion rings whole.

Zucchini in Cheese Sauce

Dear Norma/
We grow our own zucchini and it grows like crazy. We give a lot away and eat it often. I've run out of ideas of how to use it as fast as it grows. Any new ideas?

Answer/
You can make a nice small casserole (or a big one by doubling this recipe) baking it in a cheese sauce.

3 small zucchini	1 egg
Salt	2/3 cup grated cheese
1/4 cup milk	4 tbsp. butter

Wash zucchini and cut into 1/2-inch slices. Cook in small amount of salted water for one minute. Drain. Pre-heat oven to 400F. In small bowl, beat the egg. Add milk and grated cheese and mix well. Put zucchini in a buttered casserole and pour the cheese mixture over it. Top with butter and bake, uncovered until cheese is melted and top is nicely browned. Scatter croutons on top for last two minutes of baking if desired.

Zucchini Cheese Pie   *Serves 6 to 8*

Dear Norma/
Could you please give us a recipe for using grated zucchini in a pie one could serve as a main-course luncheon dish?

Answer/
When the zucchini garden runs wild, there are never enough ways of using these little (or big) Italian-type squash. This pie is quick and easy and is big enough in case company drops in.

1/4 cup chopped onion	1/4 cup vegetable oil
3 cups grated zucchini	1 tbsp. chopped parsley
2 cups grated Cheddar	4 large eggs
(I like old cheese in this)	Salt and pepper to taste
1 cup biscuit mix	

Sauté onion until soft. Combine onion with zucchini, cheese, biscuit mix, oil and parsley. Beat eggs until blended. Combine with zucchini mixture. Add salt and pepper to taste. Pour into buttered 10-inch pie plate. Bake at 375F for 40 minutes.

Tomato Side Dish   *Serves 6*

Dear Norma/
My family loves tomatoes and I am hoping you can suggest a casserole dish using canned tomatoes, without pasta or meat. Something I can serve as a side dish with the meat served separately.

Answer/
The torn slices of bread are the surprising ingredient in this tomato side dish. I am sure your family will enjoy it for a change.

2 large cans solid pack tomatoes	1/2 yellow onion, chopped
8 whole cloves	3/4 cup brown sugar
8 whole peppercorns (black)	3 or 4 slices white bread pulled
1 bay leaf (one inch long)	into dime-size pieces
Salt to taste	2 tbsp. butter

Put cloves, peppercorns and bay leaf in cheesecloth bag. Cook tomatoes, undrained, cheesecloth bag and dash of salt on top of stove, very slowly, for 30 minutes. Stir occasionally. Add onion, sugar, bread and butter. Put in greased casserole. Refrigerate until ready to bake. Remove cheesecloth bag and bake at 400F for one hour.

Glazed Parsnips   *Serves 6*

Dear Norma/
I think parsnips are the most boring vegetable ever, but my husband was raised on them and really wants me to serve them at least once a week. Help! How can I dress them up?

Answer/
Even you may learn to love the lowly parsnip if you cook them and cut them this way. Who can resist the combined flavor of cinnamon and brown sugar?

6 parsnips	4 tbsp. brown sugar
4 tbsp. butter	Pinch cinnamon

Cut parsnips in half if too big for pot. Boil until tender, 20 to 25 minutes, depending on size. Chill and peel. Cut into strips when cold. Melt butter in frying pan and add sugar, cinnamon and parsnips. Stir over low heat until parsnips are lightly browned and coated with sauce.

Roasted Potato Wedges

Dear Norma/

I need some advice on how to roast potatoes in a separate dish to serve with my roast beef. I prefer not to cook them around the roast.

Answer/

These crisp potato wedges are equally good with a roast of beef or pork. Short par-boiling is the secret of these extra-special potatoes.

4 medium sized potatoes   **Salt**
4 tbsp. melted butter

Preheat oven to 450F. Peel potatoes and cut in half lengthwise. Stand each half upright on a chopping board and slice it in thirds down its length, making three wedge-shaped pieces. Blanch the wedges by cooking them rapidly for three minutes in enough unsalted boiling water to cover them. Drain and pat dry with paper towels. With a pastry brush, butter a baking dish large enough to hold the potatoes, side by side, in a single layer. Drizzle the melted butter over the tops and sprinkle them liberally with salt. Toast in centre of oven 15 minutes; turn them and roast another 15 minutes. They should be crisp and brown.

Drunken Soldier Potatoes   *Serves 8*

Dear Norma/

I wonder if anyone else gets sick and tired of day-in, day-out family cooking? Baking, I love, but meal planning gets me down, especially potatoes. I have baked, fried, mashed and scalloped for years. Please come to my rescue and put some excitement into family potatoes.

Answer/

I feel like saying "join the club". I, too, get tired of the daily routine of three meals to plan and cook. I substitute rice, noodles or pasta often. Try these drunken soldier potatoes to relieve the boredom.

4 large baking potatoes   **Paprika to taste**
8 tbsp. butter, melted   **Salt and pepper to taste**
1 cup grated Parmesan cheese

Scrub potatoes thoroughly but do not peel.

Cut crosswise into one-inch slices and stagger them like drunken soldiers in slanted row in buttered 9x13 inch dish "sort of leaning on each other for moral support."

Pour melted butter over potato slices covering all exposed surfaces.

Sprinkle with cheese and paprika, salt and pepper to taste. Bake in 350F oven for 1 to 1 1/2 hours until deep golden brown and crispy at the edges.

For smaller family, use 8-inch square pan and only half the ingredients.

Squash Casserole

Dear Norma/
We use a lot of squash but get tired of just mashed and seasoned squash. What can I do to make it more interesting?

Answer/
Make it into a casserole with stuffing. I wouldn't serve this with a stuffed chicken or turkey because the casserole, itself, has layers of stuffing. Great with roast pork.

1/3 cup butter or margarine	3 cups yellow squash, cooked
8-oz. package stuffing mix	and drained
1 can water chestnuts, drained	Salt and pepper to taste
and sliced thinly	1 cup dairy sour cream
1 can cream of chicken soup	2 medium onions, chopped
1 small jar pimentos, drained	
and chopped	

Melt butter and pour over stuffing mix. Line casserole with half the stuffing mix. Combine other ingredients and spoon into casserole. Cover with remaining stuffing mix. Bake at 350F for 35 minutes.

Broccoli Casserole   *Serves 8*

Dear Norma/
My biggest problem in serving company meals is that my vegetables never stay hot. How can I get broccoli or green beans to the table other than lukewarm?

Answer/
I've said it so often it must sound like a broken record. Making your vegetables into casseroles ensures that they will be piping hot when served. Heating the dinner plates as well as the serving dishes is a good idea, but casseroles are sure fire.

2 packages chopped, frozen	Scant cup mayonnaise
broccoli (or cook your own	(not salad dressing)
and chop it)	2 eggs, well beaten
1 cup grated Cheddar cheese	1 can condensed mushroom
Ritz crackers, crushed	soup
	Butter

Mix broccoli, cheese, mayonnaise, eggs and soup. Put in greased casserole and sprinkle with crushed Ritz crackers. Dot with butter. Bake at 350F 30 minutes.

Fish & Seafood

Salmon Coquilles *Serves 6*

Dear Norma/
　　I used to make Coquilles St. Jacques but just now I can't afford the scallops. Would it be possible to make something similar using canned salmon? I have a good supply of this on hand.

Answer/
　　The salmon coquille mixture looks attractive in the shells and is a nice change from the scallops. I sometimes use my Coquilles St. Jacques recipe and substitute scallop-sized chunks of boneless, skinless chicken breasts for the scallops. Less pricey and very tasty.

2 cans (7 3/4 oz. each) salmon	**2 tbsp. flour**
1 tsp. minced onion	**1/2 cup liquid (canned salmon**
Dash of pepper	**plus mushroom liquid)**
1 tsp. salt	**1 tbsp. lemon juice**
1 1/2 tsp. sugar	**2 tbsp. sherry**
1/2 cup sliced mushrooms	**1 tbsp. cream**
1 large peeled tomato, seeded	**1 cup soft bread crumbs**
and cut into 3/4 inch pieces	**2 more tbsp. melted butter**
1/4 cup butter	

　　Remove skin and bones from salmon and put fish in mixing bowl. Add minced onion, pepper, salt, sugar and mushrooms. Gently sauté tomatoes in the quarter cup butter for two minutes. Skim tomatoes out and add to salmon mixture. To butter in pan add flour and blend over heat. Stir in liquid, lemon juice, sherry and cream until smooth and thickened. Add to salmon mixture. Spoon into six unbuttered individual shells. Mix crumbs with melted butter and sprinkle evenly over top. Bake at 350F 20 minutes or until bubbly around edges.

Buffet Salmon Casserole   *Serves 8*

Dear Norma/
    Our family has a tradition of serving fish on the day following a holiday dinner. It is a welcome change after all that turkey and ham. Could you suggest a casserole that would serve eight?

Answer/
    This recipe comes from Vancouver where there are probably more and better salmon recipes than anywhere else.

16 oz. canned sockeye salmon	**1/2 tsp. salt**
8 slices bread	**3 cups whole milk**
1/2 cup mayonnaise	**4 eggs, slightly beaten**
1 large green pepper, finely chopped	**10-oz. can condensed cream of mushroom soup**
1 medium onion, finely chopped	**1/2 cup grated old Cheddar cheese**
3/4 cup chopped celery	

Drain salmon and remove black skin. Flake fish. Mash bones and include them. Cube four slices of bread and place in bottom of large buttered baking dish. Mix together salmon, mayonnaise, green pepper, celery, onion and salt. Spread over bread. Trim crusts from remaining four slices of bread and place on top of salmon mixture. Mix eggs and milk together and pour over bread and salmon.

Refrigerate several hours. Bake at 325F 15 minutes. Remove from oven and spoon mushroom soup (undiluted) over top. Sprinkle with grated cheese (more than 1/2 cup if you like cheese) and return to oven to bake for one hour.

Dorothy's Easy Shrimp Lunch   Serves 4

Dear Norma/

I'm making a loose-leaf recipe book of easy luncheon dishes to serve four or six. I'd love to have a contribution from Stoveline, one with shrimp if possible.

Answer/

I copied down this recipe at a kitchen table in a mobile retirement village in Spanish Lakes, Florida, one winter when we were visiting Muskoka friends. We had enjoyed it for lunch and I've served it many times since.

1/2 cup chopped onion	1/2 tsp. curry powder
1 tbsp. butter	2 cups cooked shrimp, not
10-oz. can cream of shrimp	canned
soup	3 cups hot cooked rice
1 cup sour cream	

Cook onion in butter until limp. Add curry powder and cook for one minute. Add soup. Stir until smooth and hot. Stir in sour cream and shrimp and heat but don't boil or sour cream will curdle. Serve over hot rice.

Salmon Casserole with Cheese *Serves 6*

Dear Norma/
My husband doesn't care for rice so I use pasta instead in some of my casseroles. I'd like a family-size salmon casserole using some form of pasta.

Answer/
The Vancouver Aquarium book of seafood recipes has this one which uses small macaroni.

16 oz. canned salmon, drained and flaked	Pinch garlic powder
1 cup uncooked small macaroni	1/4 tsp. Tabasco sauce
	1 1/4 cups milk
5 tbsp. melted butter	1/2 pint sour cream
1/2 cup finely-chopped onion	1 1/2 cups grated Cheddar cheese
3 tbsp. flour	2 medium tomatoes
1/4 tsp. pepper	1/2 cup salted cracker crumbs

Preheat oven to 400F. Cook macaroni in salted water until tender and drain thoroughly. Melt three tablespoons butter in fry pan and sauté onion in it until tender. Add 1/4 cup water; blend in flour, pepper, garlic and Tabasco sauce. Gradually stir in milk. Cook over medium heat stirring constantly, until sauce is smooth and thick. Remove from heat and stir in sour cream and cheese.

In greased two-quart casserole, layer the macaroni, salmon and sauce mixture and repeat layers, ending with sauce. Cut tomatoes into thick slices and arrange on top. Combine cracker crumbs and remaining butter and sprinkle over tomatoes. Bake at 400F 20 minutes or until bubbly hot and nicely browned.

Hungarian Fish Fillets for Two

Dear Norma/

As soon as the holiday season is over my sister and I eat nothing but fresh fruit and fish. In two weeks we find we can take off any pounds that have snuck on with all the feasting. Can you help with a low-calorie way to cook fish fillets?'

Answer/

What a good idea. Seasonings give these fillets flair without adding calories.

1 lb. fish fillets (any kind)	1 tbsp. dried paprika
1/2 tsp. salt	1/8 tsp. cayenne
1 tbsp. lemon juice	1/2 cup buttermilk
1 tbsp. dried onion flakes	

Place fresh fish in baking dish. Sprinkle with salt (optional) and lemon juice. Bake at 400F five minutes. Combine rest of ingredients and pour over fish. Return to oven for five to eight minutes longer, or until fish flakes easily with a fork.

Crispy Fillets

Serves 4

Dear Norma/

I try to eat fish several times a week because I have read that this is good for you. I don't use any salt in my cooking. Could you give me a way of coating the fish and doing it in the oven with a minimum amount of fat?

Answer/

You are on your way to healthy eating if you cut down salt and fat. Years ago, everyone was cooking chicken pieces in the oven with this simple method and it makes nice, crispy fillets as well. The dash of fresh pepper makes up for the absence of salt.

1 lb. fish fillets	**1/2 cup corn flake crumbs**
Dash freshly ground pepper	**1 tbsp. vegetable oil**

Cut fillets into serving-size pieces, season with pepper and coat with crumbs. Spread cookie sheet with vegetable oil. Arrange fish in single layer on cookie sheet. Bake in preheated 475F oven for 10 minutes without turning.

If doing chicken pieces this way, lower oven heat to 350F and cook about 40 minutes.

Hot, Crispy Salmon Pitas

Serves 2

Dear Norma/

My husband and I eat a lot of canned salmon in the summer because we enjoy it, it's convenient and we know it's good for us. Could you suggest a different lunch dish?

Answer/

Substitute pita bread for sliced bread and it will give you an interesting and tasty lunch.

7 1/2-oz. can salmon	1/4 cup slivered almonds,
1 green onion, chopped	toasted
1/2 cup sliced celery	Salt and pepper
1/2 large tomato, seeded and	2 pitas
coarsely chopped	2 tbsp. butter or margarine
1/2 cup grated Swiss or Edam	
cheese	

Drain salmon and reserve liquid. Break salmon into chunks, mash bones and combine with liquid from salmon, onion, celery, tomato, cheese, almonds and salt and pepper to taste. Melt half of butter in frying pan over low heat. Cut four-inch slit along edge of each pita. Ease open and fill each with half the filling. Brush one side with melted butter. Place unbuttered side down in the pan. Cook until golden brown. Turn and brown other side. Repeat with second pita. Serve at once.

Chinese-type Broiled Fish Fillets   *For 4*

Dear Norma/
I would like to cook fish more often (my husband and kids love it) but I hate cleaning up the fishy fry pan and always think I can taste fish when I use the pan for other cooking. Can you give me a recipe using foil to avoid this smelly kitchen task?

Answer/
This recipe for four can be cut in half for twosome families. It's fast, easy and tasty. Just wrap the foil and pitch it after dinner.

1 lb. fish fillets	2 tsp. soy sauce
(fresh or frozen)	1 tsp. ground ginger
1 tbsp. white vinegar	1 clove garlic, crushed
1 tbsp. vegetable oil	

Mix vinegar, oil, soy sauce, ginger and garlic in a small bowl. Line a shallow baking dish with foil, letting foil come up on all sides of pan so that no juices leak into the baking dish. Place fillets in single layer on the foil. Brush fish with ginger-soy mixture and place under pre-heated broiler. Broil for three to five minutes, basting twice, just until fish is no longer translucent and flakes easily when tested with a fork. Remove to heated plates, lift out foil and discard.

Scallops on Skewers   *Serves 4*

Dear Norma/
Could you tell us how to do large scallops on skewers on the barbecue? I find scallops so expensive so I would like to combine them with some vegetables.

Answer/
Cooking scallops this way can stretch half a pound to feed four.

1/2 lb. large scallops	Salt and pepper
25 large mushrooms	3 tbsp. water
2 stems broccoli, cut in	Juice of half a lemon
one-inch pieces	3 tbsp. garlic butter
2 large carrots, sliced	

Slice carrots, cut broccoli in one-inch pieces and blanch these vegetables in salted boiling water for four minutes. Drain and set aside. Butter saucepan and add scallops. Pour water and lemon juice over fish. Season with salt and pepper. Seal inner pan with waxed paper and cover; cook scallops over medium heat for two minutes. Remove scallops from pan and discard liquid.

Place ingredients on skewers in following order: piece of broccoli, carrot, scallop, mushroom. Repeat process until all ingredients are used. Season with salt and pepper and brush with melted garlic butter. Place skewers on barbecue and cook two minutes on each side. Serve with lemon wedges.

Casseroles

Addie's Chicken Casserole　　　*Serves 8*

Dear Norma/

So many casseroles call for cooking the macaroni or other pasta before assembling the casserole. Is there any reason why the pasta can't go in raw and cook in the liquid of the casserole?

Answer/

You'd have to adjust the amount of liquid in the casserole because the raw pasta would gobble up the amount of liquid called for in recipes calling for cooked pasta and leave the casserole dry. But this recipe was designed to be used with raw macaroni so it stays moist.

2 chicken breasts and two
　thighs cut in good-sized
　chunks
1 tin condensed cream of
　mushroom soup
1 tin condensed cream of
　chicken soup

2 1/2 cups milk
7 1/2 oz. elbow macaroni (raw)
1 small package Velvetta cheese
　cut in cubes
Salt and pepper to taste
　(ground fresh pepper is best)

Mix everything together in large bowl. Transfer to 9x14x2-inch pan and refrigerate overnight. Bake, covered, at 350F one hour. Remove cover and continue baking until browned. Note: After removing cover, you could top with seasoned croutons or a can of french-fried onion rings.

Chicken Almond Company Casserole

Dear Norma/
 I'm looking for something different and fancy to serve to weekend guests from England. How about a chicken casserole to serve 8 to 10?

Answer/
 This is easy because everything except the chicken comes in cans or packages. If you'd sooner use boned and skinned chicken breasts, poached, you'll need 8 to 10 breasts. But I think the whole chicken has more flavor.

2 cooked chickens, boned and cut into bite-sized pieces OR 8 to 10 boned chicken breasts, poached and cut as above
1 package Uncle Ben's Wild Rice with Herbs, cooked in 2 1/2 cups broth from the chicken
2 cans french-style green beans, drained

1 1/2 cups Hellman's mayonnaise (don't substitute)
2-oz. jar pimientos, chopped
1 onion, chopped
1 can water chestnuts, drained, rinsed and sliced
1 can cream of celery soup
1 cup slivered almonds, toasted
Parmesan cheese
Paprika

Mix all ingredients in large mixing bowl and then put into large buttered casserole. Sprinkle generously with Parmesan cheese and paprika. Bake, uncovered, in 350F oven for 40 minutes or until bubbly hot. If desired, sprinkle generously with croutons for last 15 minutes.

Busy Day Salmon Treat   Serves 4

Dear Norma/
My husband loves salmon dishes and I love casseroles so we are hoping you have some easy recipes to suggest. Must we use the expensive red salmon in these dishes?

Answer/
Not at all. Pink salmon is quite acceptable in casserole dishes, fish cakes or a salmon loaf. These casseroles won't take too long to prepare.

1 1/2 cups noodles, cooked in unsalted water	1/2 cup evaporated milk
10-oz. can cream of mushroom soup	1 cup grated Cheddar cheese
	1 onion, chopped
	7 1/2-oz. can salmon

Toss all ingredients lightly together in casserole and top with buttered crumbs. Bake until bubbly at 425F, about 15 or 20 minutes.

Salmon Supper Casserole   Serves 4

2 cups cooked salmon	Salt and pepper
1 large onion, thinly sliced	1 cup whole milk
4 medium sized potatoes	Flour, butter

Remove bones and skin and flake fish. Spread one cup fish in buttered casserole. Cover with thin slices of onion and generous layer of sliced raw potato. Sprinkle with salt and pepper and dredge with flour. Repeat these three layers and pour in milk. Dot with butter and bake for 50 minutes at 400F or until potatoes are tender.

Seafood Lasagna   *Serves 8*

Dear Norma/
I am having some house guests for a weekend and they are both vegetarian. One of my specialities is lasagna and I am hoping there is some way I can make this with seafood instead of meat. Can you help me?

Answer/
Half the fun of cooking is being inventive and there is no reason lasagna has to have meat in it. Try this version with canned crab and cooked shrimp.

8 lasagna noodles	2 (10-oz.) cans cream of
2 tbsp. butter	mushroom soup
1 cup chopped onion	1/3 cup milk
8-oz. package cream cheese,	1/3 cup dry white wine
softened	5-oz. can crab meat
1 1/2 cups creamed	1 lb. shelled, deveined cooked
cottage cheese	shrimp
1 egg, beaten	1/4 cup grated Parmesan cheese
2 tsp. basil	1/2 cup shredded sharp
1/8 tsp. pepper	Cheddar cheese
1/2 tsp. salt	

Cook noodles. Place four in a 9x13x2-inch pan. Cook onion in butter. Add cream cheese, cottage cheese, egg, basil, salt and pepper. Spread one half of mixture over noodles. Combine soup, milk, and wine. Stir in crab and shrimp. Spoon half of mixture over cheese layer. Repeat all layers. Sprinkle with Parmesan and bake, uncovered, in 350F oven for 45 minutes. Top with grated sharp Cheddar cheese, brown under broiler and let stand 15 minutes before serving.

Small Tuna-Broccoli Casserole   *Serves 4*

Dear Norma/
I'm looking for a new tuna casserole for a small family, preferably one using some vegetables.

Answer/
This tuna casserole is packed with protein and the broccoli spears make it colorful. Try it with salmon some time.

7 oz.-can solid pack tuna,
  drained and flaked
2 lbs. fresh broccoli, sliced into
  fine spears
1/2 lb. mushrooms sliced
4 tbsp. margarine
4 tbsp. all-purpose flour
1 cup light cream

1 cup chicken broth
  (use bouillon cube)
Salt and pepper to taste
1 tbsp. chopped parsley
2 hard-cooked eggs, sliced
1/4 cup grated Parmesan
  cheese

Cook broccoli until tender crisp and arrange in bottom of shallow casserole. Lightly sauté mushrooms. Melt butter, blend in flour and stir in cream and broth to make smooth sauce. Season to taste. Gently stir in parsley, tuna, eggs and mushrooms. Pour carefully over broccoli and top with cheese. If you don't like Parmesan, top with grated Cheddar cheese. Bake 20 minutes at 350F and then put under broiler briefly to brown.

Lazy Jane's Weekend Casserole

Dear Norma/
I have that recipe using stewing beef, dried onion soup mix and mushroom soup. I would like something similar in which you don't have to brown the meat and you don't need the packaged and tinned soups.

Answer/
How about Lazy Jane's Weekend Casserole? It is considerably less expensive because you skip the commercial soups.

2 lbs. stewing beef cut into two-inch chunks	1/2 cup sifted all-purpose flour
1 cup dry red wine	3 cups water
1 1/2 tsp. salt	1 tsp. black pepper
2 medium onions, sliced	1/2 cup fine dry bread crumbs

Combine beef, wine, water, salt, pepper and onion in large casserole. Mix flour with crumbs and stir into casserole mixture. Cover. Bake in preheated 300F oven for three hours or until beef is tender. If you like, you can add half a pound sliced mushrooms for the last half hour of cooking. Freezes well.

Hobo Casserole   Serves 6

Dear Norma/
I have used all my own ground beef recipes so often that the whole family is sick of them. Can you suggest a new one, preferably with tomatoes?

Answer/
My four boys used to like this Hobo casserole and I liked it because it stretched a pound of meat to serve six.

2 potatoes, sliced	2 cups grated sharp cheese
1 onion, sliced	1/2 cup chopped celery
1 lb. medium ground beef, browned	19-oz. can stewed tomatoes
1 cup cooked rice	Bread crumbs
	Butter or margarine

In large greased casserole, layer potatoes, onion, beef, rice, one cup cheese, celery and salt and pepper to taste. Put tomatoes and cheese over that. Top with buttered bread crumbs or croutons. Cook covered for 30 minutes, then uncovered another 30 minutes, at 350F.

Potluck Special

Dear Norma/
It's like the Dirty Thirties all over again with people (like us) out of work and struggling to make ends meet. I'm sure there are lots of others like ourselves who would appreciate lots of new ways to stretch a pound of regular ground beef to feed a family.

Answer/
Combining meat with some form of pasta stretches it well. Try this Potluck Special on your family.

1 lb. regular ground meat, browned	**1/4 tsp. garlic powder**
	Pepper to taste
10-oz. can vegetable soup	**1/2 tsp. salt**
1/2 cup water	**1 tsp. Worcestershire sauce**
Large can stewed tomatoes	**1 cup macaroni, cooked**
1/2 tsp. dry mustard	**1/2 cup grated Cheddar cheese**

Brown meat in frying pan. Add vegetable soup, water, tomatoes, mustard, garlic powder, pepper, salt, Worcestershire sauce and cooked macaroni. Mix and place in two-quart casserole. Bake at 350F for 30 to 40 minutes. Top with grated cheese. Return to oven to brown. Freezes well.

Note: If the budget is really tight, leave out the cheese and top casserole with buttered bread crumbs.

Baked Cheese and Noodles   *Serves 4*

Dear Norma/

I'm a working mother (outside the home) and prepare my evening meal the night before. Could you give me a recipe for a casserole I could put together in the evening and pop into the oven when I get home at 5 p.m.? We don't eat a lot of meat.

Answer/

I'm sure there are many women like you who like to have the evening meal ready when they come home from work, so here are a couple of dishes that should fit the bill.

4 oz. uncooked medium noodles	1/2 tsp. Accent
2 tbsp. margarine	1 tbsp. flour
2 tbsp. chopped onion	2/3 cup milk
2 tbsp. chopped celery	1 cup cottage cheese
2 tbsp. chopped green pepper	1 tbsp. lemon juice
1 tsp. salt	1 tsp. dried parsley flakes
Dash pepper	2 eggs, slightly beaten

Cook noodles in boiling water about five minutes. Drain well and rinse. Drain again. Melt margarine in heavy pot. Sauté onion, celery and pepper until just tender. Add seasonings and flour and blend. Stir in milk to make a smooth sauce. Combine noodles, sauce, cottage cheese, parsley flakes, lemon juice and eggs. Pour into small buttered casserole dish and bake at 350F for 30 to 40 minutes or until firm in the middle. Can be assembled ahead and refrigerated. When needed, remove from refrigerator and let warm up in kitchen about half an hour before putting in oven.

Winter Casserole   *Serves 4 to 5*

1 tbsp. chopped onion	1/2 tsp. salt
1 tbsp. margarine	10 1/2-oz. can condensed
2 cups Uncle Ben's Quick Rice	cream of mushroom soup
1/4 cup chopped parsley	3/4 cup hot water
3/4 plus 1/4 cup shredded,	1/4 cup sliced almonds,
sharp Cheddar cheese	optional but nice

Sauté onion in margarine. Add rice, parsley, 3/4 cup cheese, salt, soup and water. Mix well. Spoon into 1 1/2 quart greased casserole and cover. Bake at 375F until rice is tender and liquid absorbed, about 30 minutes. Sprinkle top with remaining cheese and almonds and broil until cheese is melted.

Casserole for Two

Dear Norma/

I wonder if you have any idea how many live-alones and twosome readers you have? So many of your recipes are geared to large families. Could we sometimes have some small-serving recipes?

Answer/

Stoveline answers readers' requests and most come from men and women who are cooking for four-to-six member families. Here is a nutritionally balanced casserole for two. For one, put it in two individual dishes and freeze one for later use.

1 can (8-oz.) cut green beans	1 cup small curd cottage
1/2 lb. ground beef	cheese
1/4 tsp. salt	1/2 cup tomato sauce
Dash of pepper	1 green onion, finely chopped
1 cup fine-cut noodles, cooked	1 tbsp. Parmesan cheese

Drain beans. Combine beef with salt and pepper and brown in skillet. Stir in beans, noodles and Parmesan cheese. Place in two small casseroles. Mix cottage cheese with onion and tomato sauce. Spoon over top of casseroles. Bake in 350F oven for about 20 minutes or until bubbly hot.

Sprouts and Beef Casserole   *Serves 6*

Dear Norma/
I want to use more bean sprouts in my cooking but aside from adding them to stir-fry dishes I have no idea how to use them. Could you give me a recipe for a casserole combining the sprouts with beef?

Answer/
I was tossing bean sprouts into a stir-fry one day, tips and tails and all, when a guest told me that in Chinese homes these end bits were removed before cooking. Who has time to do this? Apparently it is a job given to the little old grandmother who is no longer able to cook and it makes her feel needed.

1 1/2 cups bean sprouts	10-oz. can cream of mushroom
1 onion, chopped	soup
1 cup celery, chopped	10-oz. can cream of chicken
1 cup sliced mushrooms, fresh	soup
or canned	1 1/2 cups water
3 tbsp. butter	1/8 cup soy sauce
1 lb. raw regular ground beef	Dash pepper
1/2 cup raw rice	

Sauté sprouts, onion, mushrooms and celery in butter. Place in large casserole dish. Fry ground meat and pour off grease. Add rice, soups, water, pepper and soy sauce. Add to vegetables in casserole. Bake at 350F, covered, for 30 minutes and uncovered for 30 minutes.

Company's Coming Casserole

Dear Norma/

I find the hardest part of meal preparation is deciding how to make vegetables more appetizing. Have you any new ideas for serving broccoli and cauliflower?

Answer/

I'm always happiest to meet these vegetables when they are served piping hot from the oven, fragrant with cheese, nestled in a hot mushroomy sauce and crunchy with croutons.

2 cups fresh broccoli	1 can condensed cream of
2 cups fresh cauliflower	mushroom soup
2 eggs	1 cup old Cheddar cheese,
1/2 cup good mayonnaise	grated
1 medium onion,	1/2 cup butter, melted
finely chopped	Seasoned croutons

Preheat oven to 350F. Cook vegetables in boiling, salted water 10 minutes. Drain and distribute evenly in lightly buttered large, shallow casserole. Beat eggs, combine with mayonnaise, onion, soup and half the cheese. Pour evenly over vegetables. Sprinkle remaining cheese over top and level gently with spoon. Pour melted butter over top of casserole. Cover with croutons and bake 40 minutes until bubbly hot.

Casserole of Rice
Serves 8-10

Dear Norma/
  I don't have much success cooking rice and would like an easy recipe to serve with meatballs at a buffet supper for eight people.

Answer/
  A casserole of rice done in the oven is great for a buffet supper because it takes care of itself and comes piping hot to the table.

1/4 cup butter	3 bunches green onions, and
1 cup finely chopped celery	tops, finely chopped
2 sweet red peppers, deveined	2 cups long grain rice
and finely chopped	4 (10-oz.) cans undiluted,
10-oz. can whole mushrooms,	condensed consummé
drained	Chopped fresh parsley

  Preheat oven to 350F. Melt butter in large frying pan. Add celery, red pepper, mushrooms and onion. Cook until vegetables are slightly softened, about four minutes. Stir in rice and cook, stirring, one minute. Transfer to large casserole. Stir in condensed consummé and parsley. Cover and bake 1 to 1 1/2 hours or until liquid is absorbed.

Apricot Glazed Chicken
Serves 4

Dear Norma/
  My family loves chicken with a sweet fruit sauce but won't eat it if I make it with tomatoes and spices. Would you be able to supply a nice recipe using apricot jam and chicken thighs?

Answer/
  I don't think they will object to this recipe because the seasonings are needed to counteract the sweetness of the apricot jam.

8 chicken thighs	1/2 envelope instant onion
3/4 cup apricot jam	soup mix
1/2 cup bottled Russian dressing	

  Arrange chicken thighs (or breasts) in rectangular dish. Combine other ingredients and spoon over chicken. Cook uncovered in 350F oven for 40 minutes. Serve with rice or noodles.

Mushroom Casserole *Serves 12*

Dear Norma/

I want to serve a mushroom casserole at a buffet party I am giving in the holidays. Could you give me a recipe using fresh mushrooms? I would like it to serve 12.

Answer/

Those who are cooking for fewer guests could easily cut this recipe in half. Be sure to use nippy cheese to make up for the blandness of the other ingredients.

3 lbs. fresh mushrooms
3 cups homogenized milk
1 cup sweet red pepper, diced
2 cups buttered soft bread
  crumbs

4 tbsp. butter
4 tbsp. flour
2 cups nippy Cheddar cheese,
  grated

Wash mushrooms carefully, making sure water doesn't get into undersides. Coarsely slice them. Make cream sauce from butter, flour and milk. Season with salt and pepper to taste. Arrange mushrooms, cheese and red pepper in layers in greased casserole. Pour cream sauce evenly over layered mushrooms and top with buttered bread crumbs. Bake in 350F oven, uncovered, for 30 minutes or until bubbly hot through.

Meat

Quick Fry Pan Meat Loaf — *Serves 4*

Dear Norma/

I have heard that a meat loaf can be made without an oven, on top of the stove in a cast-iron frying pan. Could this actually turn out like a meat loaf?

Answer/

Many wonderful dishes can be made in a well-seasoned cast-iron frying pan. Mine is well over 50 years old and I wouldn't trade it for anything else in my kitchen, not even my food processor. Here is the way to make a stove top meat loaf.

1 lb. lean ground beef	1/4 tsp. pepper
1/2 cup soft bread crumbs	1 small onion, finely chopped
(crumble a hamburg bun)	1/2 cup chopped celery
1 tsp. Worcestershire sauce	1/4 cup chopped green pepper
1/2 tsp. garlic powder	1 cup tomato sauce
1/2 tsp. thyme	1 tbsp. vegetable oil
1/2 tsp. salt	

In a medium-size bowl, combine beef, bread crumbs. Worcestershire sauce, garlic powder, thyme, salt, pepper onion, celery, green pepper and 1/4 cup of the tomato sauce. In heavy, medium-size skillet (preferably cast iron), heat the oil. Add the meat mixture and press to distribute evenly. Cover and cook over medium heat 20 to 25 minutes, until meat is cooked through. Invert meat loaf onto platter. (It comes out if you run a dinner knife around the edge first). Add rest of tomato sauce to skillet and bring to a boil. Pour over meat loaf.

Gone-All-Afternoon Stew   *Serves 8*

Dear Norma/
   I cook for a family of hungry teenagers and a husband who will eat anything. I need hearty recipes. My job is from 1 to 5 p.m. so I need a casserole I can put in the oven before I leave for work that would be ready for 6 p.m. dinner.

Answer/
   Try this gone-all-afternoon stew. If you don't cook with wine, substitute 2 tablespoons lemon juice in a quarter cup of water. The meat needs some acid to tenderize it.

2 lbs. beef stew meat, cubed	1/4 cup red wine
2 medium carrots, sliced	1/2 cup water
2 onions, chopped	Salt and pepper to taste
3 potatoes, quartered	1 bay leaf (optional)
1 can condensed tomato soup	

   Put everything in big Dutch oven or roasting pan. Cover and bake at 275F for five hours. The meat will be tender, and the gravy will make itself. You can toss in a can or two of mushroom pieces for the last half hour if you like.

Five-Hour Stew

Dear Norma/
   I have a part-time job, working afternoons, and hope you have that recipe for five-hour stew. It could go into the oven when I leave for work and be ready to serve when I get home.

Answer/
   This recipe has been around, in several versions, for many years. It's a handy meal-in-a-dish and it is really great to come home from work, open the door and have the stew aroma greet you.

1 1/2 lbs. cubed chuck beef	4 or 5 chopped carrots
10-oz. tin mushrooms	2 chopped onions
4 stalks celery, chopped	7 1/2-oz. tin tomato sauce
2 beef bouillon cubes dissolved	4 tbsp. minute tapioca
in one cup boiling water	Salt and pepper to taste
2 tsp. Worcestershire sauce	

   Mix everything together. Put into covered casserole or roaster and pop into 250F preheated oven. Five hours later it's ready.

Quick Beef Stroganoff — *Serves 4*

Dear Norma/
I am not a very experienced cook but my new husband wants to invite another couple from work for dinner. I will buy rolls and can make a good tossed salad but I need an easy main dish recipe.

Answer/
How about a quick beef stroganoff? Buy a package of medium noodles and follow package cooking instructions. A can of chocolate sauce, some chopped nuts and ice cream will make an easy dessert. Good luck!

1 lb. sirloin steak	Mushroom liquid plus water
1 onion thinly sliced	to make one cup
2 tbsp. butter or margarine	1 envelope brown gravy mix
10-oz. can sliced mushrooms,	1/2 tsp. paprika
drained (save liquid)	1/2 cup dairy sour cream
	Cooked noodles

Cut beef into thin strips. Sauté beef and onions in butter or margarine until meat is lightly browned. Measure mushroom liquid and add water to make one cup. Stir into beef the mushrooms, liquid, gravy mix and paprika. Simmer gently five minutes, stirring occasionally. Stir in sour cream. Heat but do not bring to boiling point. Serve over drained noodles.

Coke Steak *Serves 4*

Dear Norma/
Could my friend be pulling my leg when she tells me she cooks steaks in Coca Cola? She isn't the type you would dare ask for a recipe but I would really like to know if this is possible and what effects the cola would have on the meat.

Answer/
Years ago, I started a file of wacky-sounding recipes like Impossible Pie, Peanut Butter Stew, Mayonnaise Cake etc. and that is where I found your Coke Steak. The Coca Cola tenderizes the meat.

1 lb. round steak	1/4 cup shortening
1/2 cup flour	1 medium onion
1/2 tsp. salt	2 tbsp. ketchup
1/4 tsp. pepper	2 cups Coca Cola

Cut steak into serving pieces and dip pieces into mixture of flour, salt and pepper. Brown in hot shortening. Cover with sliced onions and add Coke mixed with ketchup. Simmer, covered, on low heat until steak is tender. If it cooks dry, add more Coke or a little hot water and continue cooking, for about 50 minutes, or until very tender.

Beef and Pork Meatloaf

Dear Norma/
I am a bit bored with my same old meatloaf recipe and hope you can come to the rescue. I would like a large loaf because we eat it hot for one meal and sliced cold the next day for sandwiches.

Answer/
Try putting some ground pork or sausage meat in this meatloaf. Along with the different seasonings, you will find this no ordinary meatloaf.

2 lbs. ground lean beef OR	1/2 tsp. dried rosemary,
1 1/2 lbs. ground beef and	marjoram or sage
1/2 lb. ground pork or	2 eggs, well beaten
sausage meat	4 slices white bread
1 large onion, finely chopped	1/2 cup milk or beef or chicken
2 tsp. salt	stock
Freshly-ground black pepper	Butter
	2 slices bacon

In large mixing bowl, combine meat with onion, salt, pepper, rosemary and eggs. Trim crusts from bread and shred bread into milk or stock. Add bread and liquid to meat mixture and blend thoroughly. Pack mixture into a lightly buttered loaf pan 9x5x2 1/2 inches mounding it slightly on top. Top with bacon slices and bake at 350F for 1 1/4 hours. Serve hot or cold.

Chinese Roast Pork   *Serves 4*

Dear Norma/
    We live on a farm and raise our own pigs and I don't mind telling you I get mighty sick of pork and wish I had a new way of roasting it. I am just a plain cook without much experience with herbs and spices so if you have a simple but different roast pork recipe, I would love to have it.

Answer/
    This Chinese roast pork is quite different and the only thing you'll have to shop for is the soy sauce and some chicken bouillon cubes.

2-lb. loin of pork, boned and rolled	**4 tsp. honey**
1/4 cup chicken stock	**1 tsp. salt**
1 tbsp. soy sauce	**1/4 tsp. powdered ginger**
4 tsp. sugar	**1/4 cup prepared mustard**
	2 tbsp. soy sauce

    Marinate meat in mixture of chicken stock, soy sauce, sugar, honey, salt and powdered ginger for two hours, turning occasionally. Roast in 325F oven for 1 to 1 1/2 hours, basting several times.

    Serve hot or cold with sauce of mustard mixed with soy sauce.

Apricot Bread Stuffing for Pork

Dear Norma/

I have two boneless pork loins in my freezer and a dinner party coming up. Can you suggest a different stuffing to put between the meat to make a really scrumptious dish?

Answer/

I like apricots with pork better than apples. Try this apricot stuffing. Depending on the size of the loins of pork, you may want to double this recipe. This is enough for three to four pounds of boned shoulder or loin of pork.

1/2 cup dried apricots	3 cups soft bread crumbs
2 tbsp. chopped onion	1/2 tsp. thyme or sage
1 tbsp. chopped parsley	Salt and pepper to taste
2 tbsp. butter or margarine	

Simmer apricots in small amount of water two minutes. Drain, cool and chop coarsely. (I use kitchen shears to cut them up). Cook onion and parsley in butter three minutes. Mix thoroughly with bread crumbs, apricots and seasonings. Taste and add more seasoning if desired.

Lay stuffing along one boned loin of pork (not the fat side). Lay other loin on top, fat side out. Tie together in several places with butcher's string. Place on low trivet or rack in uncovered, shallow pan. Roast at 325F for 3 to 3 1/2 hour (for 3 to 4 pounds of meat). Add no water, do not baste. Let stand five minutes before slicing.

Hurry-up Pork Chops

Serves 4 to 6

Dear Norma/
I would love to have a new recipe for pork chops because mine are always on the dry side.

Answer/
This is a hurry-up dinner that can be ready in 30 minutes. While chops are simmering, whip up a tossed salad and cook some rice.

4 to 6 pork chops	3 tbsp. Worcestershire sauce
1 can (10-oz.) cream of	1/2 cup chopped onions
mushroom soup	1/2 cup water

Trim most of the fat from chops. Brown chops on both sides. Mix remaining ingredients and pour over chops in frying pan. Cover and simmer 30 minutes. Serve with plain boiled rice.

Chili Baked Pork Chops

Dear Norma/
Would you have a recipe for doing pork chops in the oven, preferably with some kind of sweet and sour sauce?

Answer/
I think you'll like these baked pork chops, especially if you have some homemade chili sauce to use in the recipe.

6 pork chops	2/3 cup chili sauce
1/2 cup seasoned flour	2/3 cup water
2 tbsp. shortening	3 tbsp. brown sugar
6 slices lemon	

Heat oven to 350F. Dredge chops in seasoned flour. Heat shortening in frying pan and brown chops on each side in hot fat. Arrange in shallow baking dish. Top each chop with slice of lemon. Combine chili sauce, water and sugar and pour over chops. Cover (with foil if baking dish has no cover) and bake 30 minutes. Uncover and bake another 20 to 30 minutes, adding a little hot water if necessary.

Pork Tenderloin Medallions

Dear Norma/
Would you have a different way of cooking medallions of pork tenderloin? I would appreciate any preparation, presentation or serving ideas as well.

Answer/
While the recipe looks long, it is really very simple and always delights guests. I have also tried it with flattened portion of skinless, boneless chicken with good results.

Pork tenderloin medallions	**Seasoned flour**
Egg wash	**Flaked almonds**

Quantities will depend on how many you are serving. Put pork between two pieces of waxed paper and pound thin with rolling pin. Put flour, seasoned with salt and pepper, on one piece of waxed paper and almonds on another.

Beat egg with a tablespoon of water in a small bowl. Have ready a cookie tray. Coat each medallion lightly with flour; dip into egg, drain, and into almonds. Press almonds firmly into each piece of meat and set aside on cookie tray. When all medallions have been coated, cover with waxed paper or plastic wrap and refrigerate at least two hours. (This makes the coating stay on the meat while cooking.)

Put three tablespoons butter and one tablespoon vegetable oil into heavy skillet (the oil keeps the butter from burning) and heat. Brown a few medallions at a time on both sides until almonds are golden brown. Transfer to cookie sheet and continue until all meat is cooked. Allow two medallions per serving.

Keep hot in 300F oven for a few minutes. Serve on heated dinner plates with garnish of watercress, small new parslied potatoes and lightly-cooked snow peas. A wedge of lime should be served on each plate, to be squeezed over the pork.

Hot Dogs in Blankets   *Serves 4*

Dear Norma/
Please! A new way to serve my four kids wieners. Not in buns.

Answer/
My four boys ate these like they were going out of style and now my grandchildren gobble them up, too. I hope your children like them

1 lb. wieners	Salt and pepper to taste for
3 medium potatoes, boiled	potatoes
1 egg	1 cup cornflake crumbs

Boil hot dogs until heated through. Mash potatoes, add egg and seasonings. Roll hot dogs in potato mixture, coating evenly. Then roll in crumbs. Bake on greased cookie sheet in 350F oven for 20 minutes.

Round Steak Casserole

Dear Norma/
I'm not exactly a kitchen klutz, but I am turned off by long, complicated-looking recipes. There must be other men like me who wish recipes had only three or four ingredients so how about writing for us, once in awhile.

Answer/
Touché! I'll try to include more short recipes in Stoveline with you in mind.

1 large round steak	Beef broth consommé (use
Sliced onions	bouillon cubes)
	1 can sliced mushrooms

Cut steak in serving-sized portions. Brown in frying pan in butter or margarine. Add sliced onions and beef broth to cover. Thicken like gravy. Add can sliced mushrooms, drained. Put in casserole dish and bake at 300F two to three hours or until fork tender. Serve with mashed potatoes or rice and crusty rolls and salad.

Old Quebec Dinner-in-a-Pot

Dear Norma/
   I have taken over the cooking chores in our house for three days a week since I retired. My wife still cooks the complicated meals and I stick to one-dish suppers. Would you have one involving pork chops and potatoes?
Answer/
   How big is your appetite? I presume you are cooking for two so you may want to cut this four-chop recipe in two.

4 thick pork chops	Salt and pepper to taste
4 medium-sized potatoes, pared and sliced 1/2-inch thick	4 medium-sized onions, peeled and sliced
	2 cups milk

   Remove fat from pork chops, dice and melt fat until brown. Fry chops in melted fat over quick heat, about five minutes on each side. Put chops in bottom of casserole. Cover with potatoes and onions and sprinkle with salt and pepper. Pour milk over top. Cover and bake two hours at 350F. Uncover for last 15 minutes.

Spareribs and Sauerkraut   Serves 4

Dear Norma/
   I'm looking for an easy recipe for spareribs and sauerkraut. I had them once and have never forgotten how great they were.
Answer/
   Slow cooking is the secret of tender ribs. This dish can be cooked on the stove top or in the oven.

3 lbs. spareribs	1 tart apple, peeled, cored and sliced
3 to 4 cups sauerkraut	1 tsp. caraway seeds

   Cut spareribs into individual portions and brown in a little oil in heavy fry pan. Add juice from sauerkraut and enough water to barely cover ribs. Simmer, covered, 45 minutes. Do not let mixture boil. Add sauerkraut, pushing it down into liquids in pan. Add apple and caraway seed and cook 30 minutes to one hour longer until ribs are tender. Water should evaporate during cooking. If desired, dish may be baked in 350F oven.

Kay's Cocktail Meat Balls   *Makes 60*

Dear Norma/
  I am starting to collect recipes for my holiday entertaining. Have you a recipe for cocktail meat balls and a sauce for dunking them?
Answer/
  This recipe came to me from a food editor friend in Detroit and she says Michigan cooks request it year after year.

1 lb. medium ground beef	1/4 tsp. pepper
1/2 cup fine, soft bread crumbs	1/4 tsp. ground ginger
1/4 cup milk	1 tsp. salt
1/4 cup sherry	2 tbsp. bacon drippings or
1 egg, lightly beaten	other fat
2 tbsp. grated onion	

  Mix beef, crumbs, milk, sherry, egg, onion, ginger, salt and pepper. Shape mixture into little balls, using about one level teaspoon of mixture for each. Heat bacon drippings in large, heavy skillet; add a single layer of meat balls and cook, slowly, for 10 minutes or until meat is done, shaking pan gently from time to time to cook and brown evenly. When meat is cooked, spear each with a pick and arrange in hot serving dish. Serve with curry sauce for dunking.

Curry Sauce
  Combine one can (10-oz.) cream of mushroom soup with one-fourth cup sherry and a teaspoon or more, to taste, of curry powder. Heat through and serve with meat balls.

Roast Leg of Lamb
Serves 6 to 8

Dear Norma/

I want to serve a leg of lamb for my Easter dinner and I would like it to be perfect because my new in-laws are coming to visit for the first time. What kind of herbs or spices go best with lamb?

Answer/

Garlic, lemon and rosemary have a wonderful affinity with lamb and I am sure if you cook your lamb until just pink it will be a hit with your husband's parents.

1 leg of lamb, about 6 1/2 lbs.
3 cloves of garlic, slivered
1/2 cup fresh lemon juice
1 1/2 tsp. dried rosemary
1 1/2 tsp. coarsely ground black pepper
Salt to taste

Preheat oven to 400F. Make small slits, just large enough for the garlic slivers, evenly in the leg of lamb and insert the garlic. Rub meat all over with the lemon juice and then pat the rosemary and black pepper evenly over the surface. Sprinkle with salt to taste. Put lamb in roasting pan and put in oven. Reduce heat to 350F and roast for 1 1/2 hours for medium rare. Let stand 10 minutes before carving.

Chicken

City Chicken

Dear Norma/

For several years I have attended a dinner at a local restaurant and City Chicken was one of the menu items. We would like to make this at home if you can supply a recipe.

Answer/

This rings a bell. When I was a teenager in Moose Jaw, Sask., our family often enjoyed these mock drumsticks. I can even remember the first time I tackled making them without my mother's supervision.

1 lb. veal steak	Dry bread crumbs
1 lb. pork steak	1/4 cup butter or margarine
Seasoned flour	1 tbsp. grated onion
1 egg	Chicken stock made from one
2 tbsp. water	chicken bouillon cube

Preheat oven to 325F. Cut the veal and pork into 1x1 1/2-inch pieces. Arrange the veal and pork cubes alternately on six wooden skewers. Press the meat close together in the shape of a drumstick. Roll each in seasoned flour (I add a smidgen of sage to the salt and pepper).

Beat the egg with the water and dip the sticks of meat in the egg mixture and then roll them in the bread crumbs, pressing crumbs onto meat. Refrigerate for at least one hour so crumbs will adhere to meat.

Melt the butter or margarine in a large skillet. (I add a bit of vegetable oil so the butter won't burn). Brown the meat on all sides in hot fat and add the grated onion. Cover the bottom of the skillet with boiling chicken stock. Cover the skillet and place in oven. Bake about 50 minutes or until meat is tender. Remove cover for last 20 minutes of baking.

Sweet and Tangy Chicken   *Serves 12*

Dear Norma/
We are going to the cottage soon and one thing I want to avoid is the same old chicken pieces done on the barbecue. Would you have something completely different that could be done in the oven on a rainy day?

Answer/
The ingredients in this chicken dish may sound weird, but it's delicious. Try serving it with brown rice with the gravy spooned over the rice.

4 whole chicken breasts, split	1/2 of 8-oz. bottle Russian
4 chicken leg-thighs, not split	dressing
9-oz. jar apricot jam or	1 envelope dry onion soup mix
preserves	

Place chicken in large, shallow baking pan. Combine all other ingredients and pour over chicken, coating all pieces. Bake at 350F for one hour and 15 minutes.

Chicken Pack-a-Pita

Dear Norma/
I see those pita breads in the supermarket and wish I knew what to do with them. I need an actual recipe. People just tell me, "Oh, you can stuff them with anything." Not me. I need directions. Please help.

Answer/
Try this chicken pack-a-pita. You'll love it. Another time substitute canned salmon or chunk tuna, leftover roast beef or pork for the chicken or turkey.

1 cup chopped cooked chicken	1 green onion, chopped
or turkey	(use part of green part)
1 cup shredded Mozzarella	1/2 cup sliced fresh mushrooms
cheese	1/4 cup canned tomato sauce
1 tomato, seeded and chopped	1/2 tsp. basil
	1/2 tsp. oregano

Combine all ingredients in a bowl. Fill pitas. Heat in 350F oven for 10 minutes or until heated through. Use to fill large or small pitas. Makes three cups filling.

Polynesian-style Chicken Legs   *Serves 4*

Dear Norma/
I have some chicken legs and thighs in my freezer and want to use them when a dieting cousin comes to visit this summer. She writes that she prefers to eat dishes without fat. Have you any suggestions?

Answer/
Try her on Polynesian-style chicken legs. No fat in this recipe and the calorie count is low.

4 chicken legs with thighs	**1 1/2 cups water**
1/4 cup chopped onion	**4 slices pineapple packed in its**
1/2 cup soy sauce	**own juice**

Trim excess skin and fat from chicken, or if you want a really low-calorie dish, remove all skin. Combine onion, soy sauce and water. Pour over chicken in casserole and bake at 350F. Baste chicken several times with liquid in pan.

After 45 minutes, turn chicken legs and bake another 45 minutes until chicken is tender and a nice, rich brown.

Serve with pineapple slices, which have been well drained, then rolled along edges in chopped, fresh parsley.

Instead of 1 1/2 cups water, you could put liquid from pineapple in pint measuring cup and add water to make up 1 1/2 cups liquid. Use this instead of all water with soy sauce. Serve with rice.

Oven Barbecued Chicken

Dear Norma/

When summer comes, there are barbecue recipes all over magazines and newspapers, but I live in an apartment and can't barbecue outside. Can you suggest a way of making barbecued chicken in my oven?

Answer/

You will get a barbecued taste with this easy chicken recipe. Put some baking potatoes in the oven with it and cook some corn-on-the-cob and you won't miss an outdoor barbecue.

1 broiler chicken, cut up or use	1 clove garlic, minced
chicken breasts and thighs	1 tsp. rosemary
1 large onion sliced	1 tsp. salt
2/3 cup ketchup	1/4 tsp. dry mustard
1/3 cup vinegar	

Place chicken, skin side down, in single layer in buttered shallow baking pan. Top with onions. Crush rosemary in your hands to break up spikey bits which can be unpleasant in sauce if left whole.

Mix remaining ingredients in small saucepan and heat to boiling. Pour over chicken. Bake at 400F 30 minutes. Turn chicken; baste and continue cooking 30 minutes longer.

Ginger Glazed Chicken

Dear Norma/

I find boneless, skinless chicken breasts much too bland unless they have some added spiciness. Could you suggest something with soy sauce and ginger?

Answer/

You can use them both in this anything-but-bland baked chicken breast dish.

6-oz. can frozen concentrated
  orange juice
1/4 cup water
2 tbsp. soy sauce
1/4 tsp. pepper
1 tsp. salt

1 garlic clove, crushed
2 tbsp. slivered candied ginger
4 boneless, skinless chicken
  breast halves OR
1 broiler-fryer cut in serving
  pieces

Combine thawed, undiluted orange juice with water, soy sauce, pepper, salt, garlic and candied ginger. Place chicken pieces in a shallow dish and pour orange juice mixture over top. Let stand in refrigerator overnight or at least three hours, turning occasionally.

Heat oven to 375F. Remove chicken from sauce and place in baking pan. Bake about 45 minutes, brushing frequently with orange sauce mixture, until tender.

Chicken and Snow Peas   *Serves 2*

Dear Norma/
We are trying to eat less red meat and, as a result, we rely on chicken and fish. Chicken gets boring and I would love a new recipe geared to two, my sister and myself.

Answer/
Chicken is an enormously versatile food and should never be boring. Try this Chinese stir-fry.

2 chicken breasts, skinned,
boned and finely sliced
1 tbsp. cornstarch
1 tbsp. pale dry sherry
1 tbsp. soy sauce
1/2 tsp. sugar
1/2 lb. snow peas, ends
snapped off

1/4 lb. mushrooms, cleaned
and thinly sliced
3 tbsp. peanut oil
4 slices fresh ginger root,
peeled and sliced like pennies
2 green onions, including
green tops, cut in 2-inch
pieces.

Marinate the sliced chicken in marinade of the first four ingredients. Heat one tablespoon of the oil in a wok or skillet until very hot. Add vegetables and toss for two minutes. Remove to warm plate. Pour rest of oil into pan, heat and add ginger and onions. After a few seconds, add chicken pieces and stir-fry until they are firm, about two to three minutes. Return vegetables to the pan, sprinkle with half-teaspoon salt. Stir and heat briefly. Add a few toasted almonds and serve at once.

Oven-fried Lemon Chicken

Dear Norma/
My children tasted lemon chicken at a neighbor's home and have been at me ever since to make some at home. I am not an inventive cook and I need a recipe for anything I do. Help would be appreciated by my Mary, Tommy and Ian.

Answer/
There are many recipes for lemon chicken. The simplest way is to follow this recipe to where the chicken is cooked and then just sprinkle with lemon juice before serving.

But the oven method is good, too, especially if you are using breasts with bone and skin.

2 lbs. chicken breasts and thighs	1 cup fine dry bread crumbs
1/3 cup flour	Shortening or oil
1 tsp. seasoned salt	2 tbsp. lemon juice
1 tsp. thyme	1 tsp. sugar (surprise!)
Milk	1/3 cup melted margarine

Dust chicken pieces with mixture of flour, salt and thyme. Dip in milk, then in crumbs. Refrigerate one hour so crumbs will stay on during frying. In deep skillet, heat one-half inch shortening or oil until hot but not smoking.

Fry chicken on both sides until lightly browned, about 15 minutes. Arrange chicken, in one layer, skin side down, in shallow baking pan. Mix lemon juice, sugar and margarine. Drizzle half of the mixture over top.

Cover with foil and bake in 350F oven 30 minutes. Uncover, turn chicken over and drizzle with remaining mixture. Bake 15 minutes longer or until tender and crisp.

Note: I use boneless, skinless chicken breasts for this recipe because they are so much easier to eat than chicken with bones.

Celebration Chicken

Dear Norma/
So many chicken recipes today call for boneless, skinless chicken breasts. I think the other parts are more flavorful. Have you a recipe for legs and thighs done in the oven with a tasty sauce?

Answer/
Not only is this tasty, but you won't have a pan to wash.

1 envelope onion soup mix	1/2 cup ketchup
2 1/2 to 3 lbs. cut-up chicken	1/4 cup brown sugar
OR disjointed thighs and legs	1/4 cup water

Place a large sheet of aluminum foil onto a 10x15-inch cookie sheet with sides. Foil should overlap pan on all sides. Arrange chicken pieces in single layer on foil. Combine other ingredients and pour evenly over chicken. Cover with sheet of foil and seal edges to make a package. Bake in 375F oven for 50 minutes.

Chicken Casserole

Dear Norma/
I am always on the lookout for different chicken casserole recipes. Do you have a new recipe using both rice and almonds?

Answer/
Be sure to spread the almonds out on a cookie sheet and toast them in a 325F oven for about 10 minutes before adding to the casserole. They stay crunchy and give the dish a nice texture.

2 cups cooked and cubed chicken	1 cup mayonnaise
1 cup chopped celery	3/4 tsp. salt
1 cup almonds, toasted	3/4 tsp. pepper
2 cups cooked rice	2 tbsp. lemon juice
2 tbsp. finely-chopped onion	2 chicken bouillon cubes in
1 can condensed cream of	1/2 cup boiling water
mushroom soup	Crushed potato chips
	1/2 cup almonds, toasted

Combine all ingredients except potato chips in big mixing bowl, tossing lightly together. Place in a greased 9x14-inch casserole dish. Top with crushed potato chips and another half cup of slivered almonds. Bake at 375F for half an hour or until bubbly hot.

Farm Mix Oven Chicken

Dear Norma/

I am all for convenience foods, especially in the summertime when we have lots of out-of-town company, but I am tired of the same old commercial mix used to shake then bake pieces of chicken. Do you know of any other quick tricks to coat chicken pieces before baking? Preferably one I can do in the morning, refrigerate and pop in the oven an hour before dinner time?

Answer/

All you need is the chicken, a package of Pepperidge Farms stuffing and some margarine and dinner is practically ready.

1 package Pepperidge Farms stuffing mix

1/2 cup melted butter or margarine
8 pieces cut-up chicken

Roll out stuffing mix to make fairly fine crumbs. Because the mix is seasoned, you won't need much salt and pepper. Dip each piece of chicken in melted margarine, then roll in crumbs until covered. Place on a cookie sheet and salt and pepper to taste. Refrigerate. This is necessary so that crumbs will stay on meat.

An hour and a quarter before dinner, place in preheated 350F oven and bake, uncovered. Voila! Crispy chicken with practically no effort.

Bread & Muffins

Jiffy Cinnamon Rolls   *Makes 12*

Dear Norma/

I can't be bothered doing yeast baking but my kids love cinnamon rolls. Could I make something similar to real cinnamon buns using baking powder instead of yeast?

Answer/

Your children likely won't know the difference when they smell the cinnamon and see the icing sugar glaze drizzled over the "jiffy" cinnamon rolls.

2 cups all-purpose flour	1/3 cup soft margarine
2 tbsp. granulated sugar	1 cup dark brown sugar,
4 tsp. baking powder	packed
1 tsp. salt	1 tbsp. cinnamon
1/4 cup cold margarine	1 /2 cup raisins, optional
1 cup cold milk	

In large bowl put flour, sugar, baking powder and salt. Cut in cold margarine until crumbly. Make a well in centre. Pour milk into well. Stir with fork to form soft dough, adding a bit more milk if needed (flours vary in dryness).

Turn out on lightly-floured board and knead eight to 10 times. Roll into a rectangle about one-third inch thick and 12 inches long.

Cream margarine, brown sugar and cinnamon together. Drop one teaspoonful into each of 12 well-greased muffin cups. Spread remaining cinnamon mixture over rectangle of dough. Sprinkle raisins over top. Roll up as for jelly roll. Cut into 12 slices. Place cut side down in muffin cups. Bake at 400F for 20 to 25 minutes. Turn out on wire rack over tray (to catch syrupy drips).

Glaze

To one-half cup icing sugar, add enough milk to make a thin glaze. Drizzle over cool cinnamon rolls.

Double Quick Rolls
Makes 12

Dear Norma/
I would like an easy recipe for a small batch of light, yeast rolls. Not more than a dozen because I live alone. I want to make some that will freeze well and that I can have on hand for guests.

Answer/
You'll love these light and airy rolls. You use a mixer so they don't require kneading. They freeze beautifully for up to four months.

1 package active dry yeast	**2 1/4 cups all-purpose flour**
(traditional)	**1 tsp. salt**
1 cup warm water	**1 egg**
2 tbsp. sugar	**2 tbsp. soft shortening**

Dissolve yeast in warm water in large mixing bowl. Stir in sugar, half of the flour and salt. Beat until smooth with electric mixer, using medium speed. Scrape down sides of bowl with rubber scraper. Add egg and shortening and beat in remaining flour until smooth. Scrape down sides of bowl again, cover with waxed paper and bath towel and let rise in warm place for 30 minutes. (I pre-heat oven slightly and let dough rise in lukewarm oven).

Stir down batter and spoon into 12 large, well-greased muffin pans, filling half full. Or you can use small disposable foil tart tins. Let rise in warm place until dough reaches top of muffin tins. Pre-heat oven to 400F during last 10 minutes of rising. Bake for 20 to 30 minutes. Remove from pans and cool on racks. Store in plastic freezer bags.

Lemon Bread

Dear Norma/

I'm having a neighborhood coffee party between Christmas and New Year's and plan to serve quick breads and hot muffins. Would you have a recipe for lemon bread, possibly with nuts, that would be a bit festive.

Answer/

My favorite lemon loaf recipe came from the 1983 Milk Calendar publishing by the Ontario Milk Marketing Board. The lemon glaze with gratings of lemon rind gives the loaves a festive air.

1 cup butter, softened	2 tsp. baking powder
1 cup sugar	1/4 tsp. salt
3 eggs separated	1 cup milk
1 lemon rind, grated	1 cup chopped nuts (walnuts,
3 cups all-purpose flour	pecans or hazelnuts), toasted

Preheat oven to 350F. Grease and flour two 8x4-inch loaf pans. Cream butter and sugar until light and fluffy. Beat in egg yolks and lemon rind.

Stir together in another bowl the flour, baking power and salt. Add to butter mixture alternately with milk, beginning and ending with flour mixture. Beat egg whites until stiff but not dry; fold into bread mixture along with nuts. Spoon into prepared loaf pans and bake for one hour or until done. Cool loaves on wire rack.

Topping

2 tbsp. soft butter	3 tbsp. lemon juice
1 1/4 cups icing sugar	1 1/2 tsp. grated lemon rind
(sift if lumpy)	

Combine butter, icing sugar and lemon juice and drizzle over cooled loaves. Sprinkle with lemon rind.

Oatmeal Brown Bread   *Makes 3 loaves*

Dear Norma/
I'm enjoying experimenting with yeast bread and rolls. A friend suggested I try porridge bread but I can't locate a recipe and hope you can help.

Answer/
This is oatmeal bread and it's wonderful. I first began making it when my four boys were growing up. The recipe said it was good toasted but it often got eaten so quickly that we didn't manage to save any for toast the next morning.

1 cup rolled oats	1/2 cup lukewarm water
2 tsp. salt	1/2 cup molasses
3 tbsp. butter or shortening	1 cup whole wheat flour
2 cups boiling water	2 cups all-purpose flour
1 envelope active dry yeast	Another 2 to 3 cups
1 tsp. sugar	all-purpose flour

Combine in large mixing bowl the rolled oats, salt and shortening. Pour in two cups boiling water. Stir until shortening melts. Cool to luke-warm.

Meanwhile, dissolve sugar in warm water, sprinkle on yeast and let stand 10 minutes until doubled in bulk. Stir briskly with fork. Add yeast mixture to lukewarm oats mixture. Add molasses.

Beat in whole wheat flour and first two cups all-purpose flour. Add second two to three cups flour, working it in with a rotating motion of the hand.

Turn dough out onto lightly floured board and knead for a few minutes. Shape into a smooth ball and place in a greased bowl, rotating dough to grease surface. Cover and let rise in a warm place until doubled, about 1 1/2 hours. Punch down and shape into three loaves. Place in greased 8 1/2x4 1/2-inch loaf pans. Bake at 375F for 60 minutes. Turn out of pan onto wire rack to cool.

Easy Monkey Bread   *Makes 1 bundt loaf*

Dear Norma/
   I like to serve hot breads or biscuits, but don't want to fuss
with yeast. What could I do with biscuits out of the supermarket dairy case that is a bit out of the ordinary?

Answer/
   Have you ever heard of monkey bread? It is usually made
with yeast dough, but this quick version uses cans of buttermilk biscuits.

3 cans buttermilk biscuits	**1/4 lb. margarine**
1/2 cup sugar	**3/4 cup sugar**
1/2 tsp. cinnamon	**3/4 tsp. cinnamon**

   Cut biscuits in quarters and roll in mixture of 1/2 cup
sugar and 1/2 tsp. cinnamon. Pile into a greased and floured
bundt pan. Melt margarine and add remaining sugar and cinnamon. Pour over biscuits. Bake in 350F oven for 30 to 35
minutes.

Lemon Cranberry Muffins   *Makes 12*

Dear Norma/
I always seem to have cranberries left over after the holidays and wonder if I could use them in muffins or a loaf.

Answer/
I buy cranberries in a five-pound bag at a cranberry marsh near Bala before we close our Muskoka cottage in October so I use the berries in cooking all winter and into the spring. Here are recipes for large muffins and a loaf of quick bread.

1/3 cup soft butter or margarine	Grated rind of one lemon
1/3 cup sugar	2/3 cup milk
1 egg, beaten	2 cups all-purpose flour
1 cup thick cranberry sauce	1 tbsp. baking powder
OR 1 1/4 cups chopped raw cranberries	1 tsp. salt

In a large mixing bowl cream together the butter and sugar. Stir in the egg, cranberries, lemon rind and milk. Sift flour, baking powder and salt into cranberry mixture and stir only until dry ingredients are moistened. Spoon into large, buttered muffin tins, two-thirds full. Bake in 400F oven for about 20 minutes.

Cranberry Nut Bread

2 cups all-purpose flour	3/4 cup orange juice
1 cup sugar	1 tbsp. grated orange rind
1 1/2 tsp. baking powder	1 egg, well beaten
1/2 tsp. baking soda	1/2 cup chopped walnuts (toast
1 tsp. salt	before using)
1/4 cup shortening	1 to 2 cups cranberries

Sift together flour, sugar, baking powder and soda and salt. Cut in the shortening until mixture resembles coarse corn meal. Combine orange juice and grated rind with well-beaten egg. Pour all at once into dry ingredients.

Mix with fork just enough to dampen. Carefully fold in nuts and cranberries. Spoon into greased loaf pan 9x5x3 inches. Bake in 350F oven for about one hour or until crust is golden and toothpick inserted into centre of loaf comes out clean.

Remove from pan to wire rack to cool. Wrap in foil and store overnight for easy slicing.

Blueberry Muffins

Dear Norma/

I have lost my recipes for Blueberry muffins and Date and Orange muffins that appeared years ago in a newspaper supplement called Food and Drink. I hope you have these on file.

Answer/

When I didn't have these recipes and appealed to other Stoveline readers, a flood of recipes came in. These are from the source you mentioned.

1/4 cup soft butter	2 tsp. baking powder
3/4 cup sugar	1/2 cup milk
1 egg, well beaten	1 cup blueberries,
1 1/2 cups pastry flour	fresh or frozen
1/2 tsp. salt	

In a bowl, cream together butter and sugar, add egg and mix well. Add sifted dry ingredients alternately with milk, beginning and ending with flour. Just stir, don't beat. Fold in blueberries (drained if frozen). Fill buttered muffin tins two-thirds full. Bake in 375F oven 15-20 minutes.

Date and Orange Muffins   *Makes 18*

1 whole orange	1 1/2 cups all-purpose flour
1/2 cup orange juice	1 tsp. baking powder
1/2 chopped, pitted dates	1 tsp. baking soda
1 egg	3/4 cup sugar
1/2 cup butter or margarine	1 scant tsp. salt

Cut orange into pieces, remove seeds and drop pieces into blender or food processor. Blend until rind is finely ground. Add juice, dates, egg and butter and give another whirl in the blender. In a bowl, sift flour, baking soda and baking powder, salt and sugar. Pour orange mixture over dry ingredients and stir lightly. Drop into buttered muffin tins and bake in 400F oven about 15 minutes.

They are super.

Pecan Muffins *Makes 12*

Dear Norma/

Would you have a recipe similar to the butterscotch pecan muffins sold at muffin shops?

Answer/

Since I don't buy muffins, I have no idea what these are like, but here is a pecan muffin recipe for you to try. The dark brown sugar gives a butterscotch flavor.

2 cups pastry flour (or 1 7/8 cups all-purpose flour)	**2 eggs, lightly beaten**
3 tsp. baking powder	**1 cup milk**
1/2 tsp. salt	**1/4 cup melted butter**
1/2 cup dark brown sugar	**1/2 cup chopped pecans, toasted**

Sift flour, baking powder and salt into bowl. Add brown sugar and pecans and mix in with fingertips. In another bowl, mix beaten eggs, milk and melted butter. Make a well in the dry ingredients, pour wet ingredients into the well and stir only enough to dampen flour. The batter should not be smooth.

Spoon into greased muffin tins, having tins two-thirds full. Before baking, sprinkle muffins with mixture of white sugar, cinnamon and more chopped pecans. Bake on middle rack of pre-heated 400F oven 15 minutes.

Sugarcrunch Coffee Cake

Dear Norma/

I want to learn to make my own coffee cakes but I am a bit leery of baking with yeast. Would you have a good, foolproof recipe for a beginner?

Answer/

A yeast-raised dough must be kept cozy warm - don't let it get a chill or get overheated. My rule is to treat yeast dough the same way you would treat a newborn baby and success is guaranteed.

Note: Don't be surprised that this recipe uses both yeast and baking powder. Unusual, but it works.

1/2 package traditional dry yeast, not quick rise	1 egg, unbeaten
1/4 cup lukewarm water	2 cups sifted all-purpose flour
1 tsp. sugar	2 1/2 tsp. baking powder
1/2 cup shortening	1/2 tsp. salt
1/2 cup granulated sugar	1/4 cup milk

Put lukewarm water in measuring cup, stir in teaspoon of sugar and sprinkle dry yeast over top. Set in warm place and leave for five minutes. Yeast will rise to double its bulk.

Combine softened shortening, half cup sugar and egg. Beat until smooth. Sift flour, salt and baking powder. Add half to shortening mixture and beat well. Add yeast mixture; beat in. Add milk; beat in. Add remaining flour mixture and beat until smooth.

Spread half of dough in greased nine-inch round layer cake tin, or nine-inch square. Sprinkle half of sugary nut filling over batter; cover with rest of batter and sprinkle on remaining filling.

Bake in 350F oven 40 to 50 minutes. Serve warm or cold.

Sugary nut filling

Mix one cup firmly packed brown sugar with three tablespoons flour and one teaspoon cinnamon. Cut in three tablespoons butter or margarine and one cup chopped walnuts or pecans. Mix well.

Sauces

Salsa Mexicana
Makes 4 cups

Dear Norma/

Do you by any chance have a recipe for salsa to use with tortilla chips? I can't find it in any of my cookbooks.

Answer/

Many readers report enjoying salsa in Mexican-type restaurants, and find the product too pricey for family use. You can use this recipe with fresh tomatoes in season or with canned tomatoes during the winter months.

4 cups peeled fresh tomatoes or canned Italian plum tomatoes	**2 tbsp. finely chopped fresh parsley**
1/4 cup canned green chilies, finely chopped	**2 tsp. chopped fresh basil**
	1 tsp. thyme
1/4 cup wine vinegar	**1 tsp. oregano**
2 garlic cloves, minced	**Salt and freshly-ground**
2 tbsp. vegetable oil	**pepper to taste**

Chop the tomatoes and combine with the remaining ingredients. Chill. Serve with any suitable Mexican or Tex-Mex dish.

Cardinal Sauce
Makes 3 1/4 cups

Dear Norma/

I had a delicious sauce poured over ice cream at a friend's cottage. It was called Cardinal Sauce and used either frozen raspberries or strawberries. Could you please print this recipe if you have it?

Answer/

Cardinal sauce contains both strawberries and raspberries. Use the frozen packages with sugar added.

3 tbsp. cornstarch	**10-oz. package each frozen raspberries and strawberries, frozen with sugar**
1 1/4 cups cold water	

In saucepan, combine cornstarch and cold water until smooth. Bring to boiling point and stir until thickened and translucent, about five minutes. Stir in thawed berries and let sauce cool. Store in refrigerator.

Cumberland Sauce for Baked Ham

Dear Norma/

I often bake a ham in the summertime because it's so nice to have something in the fridge for a cold supper. Could you let me have a recipe for Cumberland sauce and one for a sweet mustard sauce to serve with the ham?

Answer/

Both of these sauces are favorites at our house. The mustard sauce is also super drizzled over a tossed salad in place of salad dressing.

1/3 cup red currant jelly	2 tsp. dry mustard
1/4 cup port or Madeira wine	1 tsp. ground ginger
1/4 cup orange juice	2 tsp. paprika
1 tbsp. lemon juice	3 tbsp. grated orange rind

Melt jelly in small saucepan over low heat. Remove from heat and add remaining ingredients, stirring until smooth. Cool. Serve sauce at room temperature or chilled over slices of baked ham. Or use the sauce as a glaze for baked ham, brushing over the ham several times during last 30 minutes of baking. Makes one cup.

Bea's Delicious Ham Mustard

2 dessertspoons Keen's dry mustard	2 eggs
2/3 cup vinegar	1 cup white sugar

Mix mustard and vinegar in small saucepan. Add eggs and sugar. Cook over low heat, whisking constantly until it thickens and bubbles just break the surface. If you overcook it, the sauce will go thin. Store in covered jar in the refrigerator.

Note: This is too good to keep to yourself. Make two batches and give one to a neighbor.

Quick Red Clam Sauce *Serves 4*

Dear Norma/

My husband is crazy about linguini with clam sauce (the kind made with tomatoes). I don't do much fancy cooking because I have a full-time job outside the home and three children. But, if this isn't too difficult, I would love to make some for his upcoming birthday.

Answer/

What a nice surprise to plan for your husband! This recipe makes four good-sized servings so, if the children are small, it should serve your family. If they are teenagers, double the recipe.

1 large onion chopped (1 cup)	1 tsp. salt
4 cloves garlic, minced	1/2 tsp. pepper
1/4 cup olive or vegetable oil	1/2 tsp. leaf basil, crumbled
2 (8-oz.) cans minced clams or	1/2 tsp. leaf oregano, crumbled
baby clams	2 tbsp. chopped parsley
6 medium-sized tomatoes,	
peeled and coarsely chopped	

To peel tomatoes, plunge into boiling water for a minute or so. Lift out and plunge into cold water. Skins will slip off readily.

Sauté onion and garlic in oil until soft. Drain liquid from clams into the same saucepan, reserving clams. Add tomatoes and seasonings; bring to a boil. Lower heat and simmer, uncovered, stirring now and again for 15 minutes or until sauce is thickened. Mix in clams and parsley and heat five minutes longer.

Cook linguini according to package directions and serve with sauce.

Chocolate Sauce Brazilian Makes 1 1/2 cups

Dear Norma/

My boyfriend is a chocolate nut. I am sure he would eat anything doused in chocolate. I need a recipe for a very dark chocolate sauce for ice cream. The canned kind isn't dark enough for him.

Answer/

Try this Brazilian chocolate sauce with dark rum. The coffee powder gives an intriguing lift to the chocolate.

5 squares (1-oz. size)
  semi-sweet chocolate
1 square (1-oz.) unsweetened
  chocolate
1 tbsp. butter
1/2 cup sugar

1/3 cup corn syrup
1/4 cup light cream
1 tbsp. instant coffee powder
  or granules
1/4 cup dark rum

In top of double boiler, over hot water, melt chocolate, butter and sugar. Stir in corn syrup and cream. Beat until smooth. Add instant coffee and stir until dissolved. In small, heavy saucepan, slowly heat rum just until vapor rises. Ignite with match. Pour into chocolate mixture, stirring with wire whisk until smooth. Serve hot.

Refrigerate leftover sauce. Heat over hot water before serving.

Note: If you don't want to use rum, increase cream to one-half cup.

Butterscotch Sauce
Makes 1 cup

Dear Norma/

During the hot weather the kids are always asking for ice cream and I can't afford anything but the least expensive brands. This gets boring after awhile and what I am looking for, hopefully from Stoveline, is two different topping recipes that don't cost too much.

Answer/

Homemade toppings are more economical than commercial toppings and the children like them just as well. One weekend at the cottage, my grandson, Michael, said, "Do you know what I like about you, Granny? You make everything yourself and don't get it out of packages and jars."

1/2 cup brown sugar, packed
1/2 cup corn syrup
1/2 tsp. salt (or less)

2 tbsp. butter (you could use margarine in a pinch)
1 tsp. vanilla

Cook the brown sugar and corn syrup together for 10 minutes. Add the salt, butter and vanilla. Stir well and put in a small jar. For a creamy butterscotch sauce, add 1/2 cup thin cream to the sugar and syrup. Cook 30 minutes in top of double boiler, stirring occasionally. Add the salt, butter and vanilla. Serve warm or cold over ice cream.

Chocolate Fudge Sauce
Makes 2 cups

1 cup cocoa or 2 oz.
unsweetened chocolate
3/4 cup sugar
1/2 tsp. salt
1 tbsp. cornstarch

1/2 cup corn syrup
1/2 cup milk
2 tbsp. butter or margarine
2 tbsp. vanilla

Mix in top of double boiler the first four ingredients. Add the corn syrup and milk. Cook for 15 minutes over hot water, stirring until thickened. Add butter and vanilla.

Peppermint Sauce
Makes 1 1/2 cups

For chocolate ice cream.

**1/2 cup crushed peppermint
  stick candy
1/2 cup sugar
1 cup water**

**1/4 cup corn syrup
1 tbsp. cornstarch
2 tbsp. water
Green food coloring**

Mix first four ingredients in saucepan. Simmer until candy dissolves. Mix water and cornstarch until smooth. Stir into peppermint syrup. Stir until thickened. Tint with green food coloring. Cool.

Mock Maple Syrup

Dear Norma/

I've lost my Mom's recipe for mock maple syrup. We used to have it on pancakes and waffles when I was growing up and we couldn't afford real maple syrup. She's gone now and I wish we had written down her good recipes.

Answer/

This is a favorite at our Muskoka cottage and is so easy to whip up.

**1 cup brown sugar
1 cup boiling water
1/2 cup white sugar**

**1 tbsp. butter
1/2 tsp. vanilla or maple
  flavoring**

Boil brown sugar and water for 10 minutes. Melt granulated sugar in cast iron fry pan over direct heat, stirring constantly, until it is slightly brown. Remove from heat and carefully add hot syrup, stirring until dissolved. Add butter and stir until melted. Cool and add flavoring. If syrup is too thick, thin with a little boiling water.

Chinese Plum Sauce

Dear Norma/

I've searched high and low for a recipe for the kind of plum sauce served in restaurants in little dipping dishes to go with egg rolls. I don't care how much trouble it is to make, I just want to make my own with your help.

Answer/

It is a bit of trouble but well worth it. The only catch is it should be sealed in jars and set aside for a month before using.

1 cup skinned, pitted plums	**1/2 cup chopped pimento**
1 cup skinned, pitted apricots	**1 cup honey**
1/2 cup apple sauce	**1/2 cup vinegar**

Skin plums and apricots by dropping them in boiling water. Turn off the heat and let stand for three minutes. The skins and pits are easily removed. (Yes, you could use drained, canned apricots when fresh apricots are not in season).

In a heavy, medium-sized saucepan with a lid, combine all ingredients. Heat to boiling; cover and simmer for one hour, stirring occasionally, until slightly thickened. If it has not thickened after one hour, remove cover and cook over medium heat, stirring until slightly thickened.

Pour into sterilized small jars and seal while still hot. Screw caps on tightly. Put aside in a cool, dark place for a month.

Note: Serve as dipping sauce for egg rolls, Chinese roast pork or barbecued spareribs.

Desserts

Heavenly Hash

Serves 8 to 10

Dear Norma/

Years ago, I had a recipe for a dessert called Heavenly Hash. Is it possible to locate this 30-year-old recipe for me?

Answer/

This was a popular bridge club dessert back in the 1950s and appeared so often that guests were wont to groan (under their breath), "Oh, not again!" But it is delicious and could stand a comeback.

1 (11-oz.) can mandarin orange sections
1 (8-oz.) bottle red maraschino cherries
1 (8-oz.) bottle green maraschino cherries
2 (8-oz.) cans pineapple tidbits
1 lb. marshmallows (large kind)
1 pint whipping cream
1/8 tsp. ground cardamom
1/4 tsp. ginger
1 tsp. freshly-grated orange peel

Drain fruit well. Cut marshmallows in half, using scissors dipped in cold water. Whip cream; add cardamom, ginger and orange peel. Gently fold all ingredients together. Refrigerate overnight before serving.

Grammy's Blueberry Pudding   *Serves 10*

Dear Norma/
We spend a good part of the summer in blueberry country and my children are good pickers. Would you have anything new by way of a blueberry pudding I could make at the cottage when the time comes?

Answer/
This is really a cake, but it's brimming with blueberries and topped with a tangy lemon sauce. Great for a cottage because it serves 10.

1 1/2 cups fresh blueberries	1 tsp. vanilla
2 tbsp. all-purpose flour	1 1/2 cups all-purpose flour
1 egg	2 tsp. baking powder
1/2 cup sugar	1/4 tsp. salt
2 tbsp. butter or margarine, softened	1 cup warm milk

Preheat oven to 350F. Grease six-cup ring mold; set aside. In small bowl, beat egg, butter, sugar and vanilla with electric beater on high speed until light and fluffy.

Thoroughly stir together 1 1/2 cups flour, baking powder and salt. Alternately add flour mixture and warm milk to creamed mixture, beating well with electric mixer on medium speed after each addition, beginning and ending with flour addition. Fold in blueberries which have been tossed with the two tablespoons flour.

Pour batter into greased mold. Bake 30 to 35 minutes or until wooden pick inserted into centre comes out clean. While pudding is baking, prepare lemon hard sauce. Cool pudding in mold 10 minutes. Invert on to wire rack and cool slightly. Serve warm with lemon hard sauce.

Lemon Hard Sauce

1/2 cup butter, softened	2 tbsp. lemon juice
1 cup icing sugar	

In small bowl, beat soft butter with icing sugar on high speed until fluffy. Beat in lemon juice. Makes 1 1/2 cups sauce.

Strawberry Mousse *Serves 6*

Dear Norma/

I'm having a problem with my bridge club. All seven members are dieting (it happens every year after the feasting of the holiday season). No one wants a fruit and cheese platter every week. Can you suggest a low-calorie dessert I could serve?

Answer/

You would have to double this recipe and do serve it in your nicest sherbet dishes. Add half a maraschino cherry (5 calories) if the dieters aren't too serious.

1 envelope unflavored gelatin	1/2 tsp. vanilla
2 tbsp. water	1 cup evaporated milk
2 cups frozen strawberries	(2 per cent)
2 tbsp. artificial liquid sweetener	

Sprinkle gelatin over cold water and set aside. Combine strawberries and sweetener and cook until berries are soft. Remove from heat. Add softened gelatin and stir until dissolved. Cool, then add vanilla. Chill evaporated milk in freezer tray until ice crystals form around edges. In large, chilled bowl, whip until stiff peaks form. Slowly pour strawberry mixture into whipped milk. Beat to combine. Pour into dessert glasses. Chill until firm.

Strawberry Nevers *Serves 6 to 8*

Dear Norma/

I make both strawberry shortcake and strawberry pie using berries from my own patch, but I'd like some new strawberry dessert ideas.

Answer/

Aren't you lucky to have your own patch? Jehane Benoit, who was a prolific writer and outstanding researcher on Canadian foods, said this was her favorite way of preparing fresh strawberries for her guests.

1 qt. fresh ripe strawberries	1/2 cup fresh orange juice
1 cup Seville orange	1 tsp. grated orange rind
marmalade (do not substitute)	1 tsp. lemon juice
1/4 cup orange-flavored	Whipped cream (optional)
liqueur or brandy	

Wash strawberries before hulling them. Drain thoroughly on an absorbent towel. Hull. Over low heat, mix marmalade with liqueur or brandy and stir until well blended. Add orange juice gradually, while stirring, until you have a medium thick sauce. Add orange rind and lemon juice.

Put the berries in a cut glass dish and pour the cooled marmalade sauce over them. Refrigerate at least two hours before serving. Serve with a bowl of whipped cream sweetened with a little marmalade and flavored with some orange-flavored liqueur or brandy. It is good without the cream, too.

Berries in Cantaloupe Shells

Another unusual way to serve strawberries is simplicity itself. Again, use your nicest glass bowl.

Cut up a big bowl of sliced fresh, ripe strawberries. Mix three tablespoons granulated sugar and three tablespoons balsamic vinegar or raspberry vinegar. Toss and serve in cantaloupe shells. Do not substitute any other type of vinegar.

Pineapple Dessert

Dear Norma/

Would you have a recipe for a nice, gooey dessert that I can make two days ahead and store in the fridge until needed? I love pineapple, but I can't cook worth a hoot, so how about an uncooked dessert?

Answer/

This dessert doesn't need any more effort than beating up a cup of whipping cream. You'll love it.

2 cups graham wafer crumbs	1 cup whipping cream
1/4 cup butter	1 cup pineapple pie filling
4 cups small marshmallows	

Whip cream and add marshmallows. Rub together wafer crumbs and butter and pat all but quarter cup into nine-inch square pan. Spread half of the cream mixture over crumbs. Spread on pineapple pie filling. Spread remaining cream mixture over pineapple filling. Top with remaining graham wafer crumbs. Refrigerate two days before serving.

Yummy Freeze

Dear Norma/

I'm all for desserts that can be made in the freezer rather than the oven in the heat of the summer. Have you some new, easy no-cook dessert ideas?

Answer/

Try this yummy freeze. It's as easy as opening a can and everyone raves about it when you serve it.

28-oz. can fruit cocktail	1/2 tsp. vanilla
Chocolate wafers	1/2 cup small marshmallows
1 cup whipping cream	1/4 cup chopped nuts
1 tbsp. sugar	1 banana, sliced

Let fruit cocktail drain through wire sieve at least 30 minutes. Line eight-inch square cake pan with chocolate wafers. Whip cream, flavor with sugar and vanilla. Add drained fruit cocktail, marshmallows, nuts and banana to whipped cream. Pour over chocolate wafers, cover with foil and freeze. Remove from freezer 15 minutes before cutting into squares to serve.

Pineapple Squares

Dear Norma/

Recently I enjoyed some pineapple squares with a short-bread base. My hostess said the recipe came from an old Monarch Flour cookbook years ago. Would you have anything similar?

Answer/

Why didn't you ask her on the spot if you could copy down the recipe? Some of my happiest moments have been spent in other women's kitchens sitting at the kitchen table scribbling down recipes they have been only too happy to share.

This won't be the recipe you are looking for, but it may be similar.

1 cup all-purpose flour	1/4 cup butter
1/4 cup brown sugar	1/4 tsp. salt

Sift flour and salt into bowl. Add sugar and blend. Add soft butter and work into dry mixture with fingertips until mixture is crumbly. Press firmly into bottom of lightly-greased nine-inch square cake pan. Bake 15 minutes at 350F.

Topping

1 egg	1 cup flaked coconut
1 cup brown sugar, packed	1/4 cup quartered maraschino
1 tsp. rum extract	cherries
1/2 cup flour	1/2 cup well-drained crushed
1/2 tsp. baking powder	pineapple
1/4 tsp. salt	

Beat egg well. Add brown sugar gradually, beating well after each addition. Beat in rum extract. Sift salt, flour and baking powder into mixture and stir to blend. Stir in coconut, cherries and pineapple. Spread over hot shortbread layer and return to oven. Bake 35 minutes until nicely browned. Cool and cut into squares or bars.

Raspberry Delight

Dear Norma/

I need a dessert recipe for a pot-luck supper at my church. I especially like those that have a graham cracker crust and something rich and sumptuous on top.

Answer/

This raspberry delight might be something different for you to take. The crumb base is a variation on the usual graham cracker crumb crust.

18 graham wafers	1/4 cup butter or margarine
1/2 cup icing sugar	1 tsp. cinnamon

Crush graham wafers into fine crumbs and add to remaining ingredients. Set aside one-quarter of this mixture for topping. Pat rest into 8x12-inch pan.

1 package raspberry gelatin	20 regular size marshmallows
1 cup boiling water	1/2 cup milk
1 package frozen raspberries, slightly thawed	1 cup stiffly-beaten whipping cream

Dissolve gelatin in boiling water. When gelatin is partially set, add slightly-thawed raspberries. Mix well and spread over crumbs. Melt marshmallows in milk over low heat. When cool, fold in whipped cream. Spread over berry mixture and sprinkle with reserved crumbs. Keep in refrigerator.

Frozen Ambrosia Squares

Dear Norma/

I'm looking for a frozen-dessert type recipe for a small luncheon party I'm giving for a June bride-to-be. I'm no great shakes as a cook so I need something that is sure to turn out.

Answer/

I've never had a failure with these frozen ambrosia squares and have been asked for the recipe dozens of times.

1/2 cup butter, room temperature	8-oz. can crushed pineapple, well drained
2 tbsp. brown sugar	1 cup whipping cream
1 cup all-purpose flour	2 tbsp. icing sugar
1/2 cup melted butter	1 tsp. vanilla
3 cups icing sugar	Maraschino cherries for garnish
1 small egg, beaten	

Cream half cup butter, brown sugar and flour together and pat into greased nine-inch square cake pan. Bake at 350F for 15 minutes until light brown only. Cool. Chill pan. Beat melted butter, icing sugar and beaten egg until smooth; spread over cooled shortbread base in pan. Pat well-drained pineapple into frosting layer.

Whip cream, add icing sugar and vanilla. Spread whipped cream over pineapple. Wrap in foil and freeze. Keep frozen until time to serve. Cut in large squares for dessert and garnish with maraschino cherry halves.

Forgotten Dessert

Serves 6 to 8

Dear Norma/

My family is strawberry crazy so we serve them at least once a day all through the growing season. There is a limit to the number of times I want to serve them as is, or crushed and sweetened over ice cream. I hope you have a really different way of using a quart of these berries.

Answer/

I'm always reminded in strawberry season of the poet who wrote, "Doubtless God could have made a better berry, but doubtless, God never did."

If your family doesn't have to count calories, I'm sure they will find this version of forgotten cookies a wonderful base for juicy, crimson red strawberries.

6 egg whites	1 tsp. vanilla
1/4 tsp. salt	1 pint whipping cream
1/2 tsp. cream of tartar	Icing sugar
1 1/2 cups granulated sugar	1 tsp. vanilla

Preheat oven to 450F. Beat egg whites and salt until foamy. Add cream of tartar. Then add, one tablespoon at a time, the granulated sugar, beating until no graininess remains. Beat in one teaspoon vanilla. Lightly grease 14x9x2-inch cake pan and spread this meringue evenly in pan.

Put in oven, turn off heat, go to bed. Do not peek!

Next morning, remove from oven. Whip one pint whipping cream, sweetened to taste with icing sugar and one teaspoon vanilla. Spread over cold meringue and refrigerate until serving time. Cut into squares and top each with whole or sliced fresh strawberries.

Teenagers can manage two servings!

Cakes

Billie's Prize-Winning Cheesecake

Dear Norma/

A few years ago you printed a cheesecake recipe that had taken first prize at the Canadian National Exhibition many years ago. It became a family favorite, but I've lost the recipe. Could we please have it repeated?

Answer/

That recipe came from Mrs. Billie Wybraniak who won many CNE prizes for her cakes and cheesecakes. She baked it in a 9x13x2-inch cake pan and cut it into one-inch squares. Serves 40.

Base

2 cups graham wafer crumbs   **1/3 cup melted butter**

Spread on bottom of foil-lined 9x13x2-inch cake pan.

Filling

3 large packages Philadelphia   **5 eggs**
cream cheese (1 1/2 lbs.)   **1/2 tsp. vanilla**
1 cup white sugar

Beat room-temperature cream cheese with electric mixer and gradually add the sugar, beating well. Add eggs, one at a time, beating after each addition. Add vanilla. Pour into prepared pan and bake for 50 minutes at 325F. Do not overbake. Temperature is very important. Take out of oven for five minutes and then put on topping.

Topping

1 large carton dairy   **1/2 cup sugar**
sour cream   **1/2 tsp. vanilla**

Mix together and pour over cheesecake and return to oven for five minutes. Cool half an hour and cut in one-inch squares.

Mrs. Wybraniak says that if cheesecake cracks, it is because the oven heat is too high and the cheesecake is baked too long. Her cake, having no flour, sets more than bakes. It must not get brown on top. If it does, it is baked too long. On being done, it will be jiggly when touched, but not wet.

Chocolate No-bake Cake *Serves 16-24*

Dear Norma/

I am looking for something new in an easy-to-make dessert to serve with coffee to my bridge club. Could you suggest something that doesn't require baking?

Answer/

You can serve thin wedges of this chocolate no-bake cake because it is so rich and satisfying. It cuts into 24 thin wedges or 16 more generous servings.

1/2 lb. vanilla wafers, crushed
1/2 cup chopped pecans
1 cup (4 oz.) chopped dried apricots
1/2 cup brown sugar, packed
Juice and grated rind of one orange

1 tbsp. cocoa
1/2 cup shortening, melted
3 squares (3 oz.) semi-sweet chocolate, melted
Extra grated chocolate and pecans to decorate

Combine cookie crumbs, nuts, apricots, sugar, cocoa, orange juice and rind in large bowl. Pour melted shortening over and mix very thoroughly. Grease an eight-inch round cake pan, then line base with an aluminum foil circle cut to fit. Grease foil.

Place mixture in cake pan and press down firmly using a flat-based glass. Chill at least an hour. Run spatula around edge of pan and turn cake out onto sheet of waxed paper. Break chocolate into pieces and melt in bowl set over (not in) simmering water. Spread melted chocolate over top and sides of cake and decorate with extra grated or curled chocolate and pecan halves. Cut in thin wedges and serve with coffee.

Joan's Apple Cake

Dear Norma/

We have our own apple trees and I am always looking for new apple recipes. Do you have a favorite apple cake recipe you could share with me?

Answer/

You'll love this cake when you make it. The recipe came to me from a friend who said it originated in Vancouver and I've been making it since 1975.

2 cups grated apple	1 tsp. cinnamon
1 cup sugar	1 tsp. baking soda
1/4 cup salad oil	1/2 tsp. salt
1 well-beaten egg	1/2 cup toasted walnuts,
1 tsp. vanilla	coarsely chopped
1 cup all-purpose flour	

Combine first five ingredients in mixing bowl. Sift together next four ingredients and combine with mixture in bowl. Add walnuts. Grease and flour a loaf pan and then line tin with greased paper so that cake will come out of tin easily. Bake at 350F for 40 to 60 minutes (until it tests done). Cool and ice.

Icing

4-oz. package cream cheese	1 1/2 cups icing sugar
1 tbsp. butter	1 tsp. rum flavoring

Have cheese and butter at room temperature. Beat all ingredients with electric mixer and ice top and sides of cake.

Julie's Buttermilk Banana Cake

Dear Norma/

I would love to have a foolproof recipe for banana cake - not banana bread. I have just acquired a food processor and would appreciate having a recipe I can make in this handy kitchen machine.

Answer/

Some of my most prized recipes are those given me by my daughters-in-law. This is Julie's banana cake recipe and I'm sure you'll love it as much as I do.

2 cups sifted all-purpose flour	**1/2 cup buttermilk**
1 tsp. baking soda	**1 1/2 cups sliced ripe bananas**
1 tsp. baking powder	**1 tsp. vanilla**
1/2 tsp. salt	**2 eggs**
1 1/4 cups sugar	**1/2 cup walnuts**
1/2 cup shortening (room temperature)	

Heat oven to 350F. Grease and flour two eight-inch round layer cake tins. Sift flour, baking powder, baking soda and salt into large mixing bowl. Put sugar, shortening, bananas, buttermilk, eggs and vanilla into blender or food processor. Cover and process at high until smooth. Add nuts. Blend only until nuts are chopped. Add to dry ingredients and mix well with spoon.

Turn batter into prepared pans and bake 35 to 40 minutes or until done. Cool on wire racks. Sift with icing sugar through a fine sieve or make into layer cake using cream cheese or butter icing.

Lumberjack Cake   *Makes 8-in. square cake*

Dear Norma/

Have you ever heard of a lumberjack cake? I would like to have the recipe to send to my daughter in Australia. She heard that the recipe came about in war time and earned its name because it was so moist and nutritious.

Answer/

Many readers sent in their versions of this recipe when I appealed for it through Stoveline. One reader wrote, "A friend in Balgowlash, Australia, sent me the recipe last winter. The newspaper "down under" claims this cake is made daily in logging camps in Northern Canada."

1 cup peeled, chopped apples	1 cup sugar
1 cup chopped dates	1 egg
1 tsp. baking soda	1 tsp. vanilla
1 cup boiling water	1 1/2 cups all-purpose flour
1/2 cup shortening or butter	1/2 tsp. salt

Combine first four ingredients in small bowl and let cool. Cream shortening and sugar, add egg and vanilla. Mix flour and salt and add alternately to creamed shortening mixture with fruit mixture. Spoon batter into greased and floured eight-inch square pan and bake in 350F oven for 50 minutes.

Topping

4 tbsp. butter	4 tbsp. milk
1/2 cup brown sugar	1 cup shredded coconut

Cook topping ingredients in small pan over low heat until sugar and butter are melted. Spread over cake as soon as it comes from oven and return to oven and bake 20 minutes more or until topping is golden brown.

The Ruby Slipper Cake

Dear Norma/
About 10 years ago, more or less, I had a wonderful recipe for Ruby Slipper Cake. It had raspberry jelly powder and sour cream or yogurt. If you happen to have this filed away I would sure like to make it again.

Answer/
Your lost cake recipe was developed by General Foods using Jell-O and Dream Whip. I had it filed under Wacky Cakes.

1/2 cup chopped pecans	2 eggs
1 package (2-layer size) white cake mix	3-oz. package Jell-O raspberry jelly powder
1 cup sour cream or yogurt	Icing sugar
1/4 cup water	Dream Whip dessert topping

Sprinkle nuts evenly over bottom of thoroughly greased (use butter) and floured 10-inch tube or fluted tube pan. Combine cake mix, sour cream, water and eggs in large mixing bowl. Blend, then beat at medium speed with electric mixer for two minutes.

Sprinkle jelly powered into 1/2 cup batter and blend. Pour one-third plain batter over nuts in cake pan. Spoon about half of jelly batter in a one-inch wide ring around centre of pan, keeping away from sides. Repeat layers, ending with white cake batter, spreading it over the jelly batter to cover.

Bake at 350F for 45 to 50 minutes (ovens vary), or until cake springs back when lightly pressed with finger. Cool in pan five minutes. Remove from pan and continue cooling on rack. Sprinkle with icing sugar through a sieve. Garnish with prepared Dream Whip dessert topping if desired and serve to the people you love.

Eva's Turtle Cake

Dear Norma/

Have you ever heard of a Turtle Cake? It is chocolate with a candy-type filling. It's not a commercial recipe, it's a home-made cake, but for the life of me I can't find the recipe.

Answer/

The United Churches in Canada Let's Break Bread Together has this recipe. I haven't tried it, but most church cookbook recipes are tried and true.

With the rich filling you won't want to ice the cake.

1 German chocolate cake mix	1 cup chocolate chips
42 caramels	1 cup pecans or walnuts (I toast
1/2 cup block margarine	nuts before using in baking)
1/2 cup Carnation milk	

Make cake batter as directed. Pour half the batter into greased and floured 9x13-inch cake pan. Bake 15 minutes. Meanwhile, melt caramels, margarine and Carnation milk in saucepan. Add chocolate chips and nuts. Spread over baked half of cake, then add rest of batter and continue baking for 20 minutes.

Tipsy Parson Cake *Serves 10*

Dear Norma/

My mother-in-law used to serve a Tipsy Parson's Cake instead of a heavy dessert like plum pudding for her Christmas dinner. She didn't leave her recipe to anyone and my husband remembers the dessert fondly. Would you have this recipe?

Answer/

This cake is a bit like a trifle but without the custard. You can either make your own sponge cake or buy it. Best to let it get a bit stale before using.

1 large sponge cake or two small ones	1/4 cup sliced blanched almonds
1 cup sherry or cognac	1 cup whipping cream, whipped and sweetened and flavored with vanilla
1/2 cup apricot or raspberry jam	

If using large sponge cake, split into two layers. Put each layer in deep dish and drizzle with half of sherry or cognac over each, making sure to moisten cake evenly. Brush each layer with jam and chill at least two hours. Stud top layer with almonds and surround with sweetened whipped cream.

Sept-Isles Fruit Cake

Dear Norma/

The best dark Christmas cake I have ever made came from one of your columns many years ago and I have lost it. I remember it came from Quebec and had strawberry jam in it. Could you possibly find it from this slight bit of information?

Answer/

That recipe came from a 1967 column and was called Sept-Isles Fruit Cake. I remember it because I still make it and because of the number of requests I have had for it over the years. It makes a 4 1/2 pound cake.

1 cup seedless raisins	2/3 cup strawberry jam
1 cup golden raisins	1/4 tsp. baking soda
1 cup currants	1 tsp. each cinnamon and
2 lbs. candied cherries, red	allspice
and green	1/4 tsp. mace
1 cup pecan halves	1/4 tsp. nutmeg
1 cup chopped blanched	2/3 cup butter
almonds	2/3 cup brown sugar, packed
1 2/3 cups sifted all-purpose	4 eggs
flour	3 tbsp. orange juice
1/3 cup molasses	1/2 cup brandy or rum

Combine all fruit and nuts. Sift flour, measure and mix 1/3 cup with fruit mixture. Sift remaining flour with soda and spices. Cream butter and sugar together until light and fluffy; add eggs one at a time, beating well after each addition. Add molasses, orange juice, brandy or rum and jam. Stir into fruit and nuts. Fold in flour-spice mixture about one third at a time.

Spoon into well-greased, brown paper-lined Christmas cake deep pan, square or round. Bake in 250F oven on middle shelf for 3 to 3 1/2 hours or until cake tests done. Place shallow pan of water on bottom shelf of oven under cake when baking starts. When done, remove from pan and cool on wire rack. Wrap in brandy or rum-soaked cheesecloth and then in foil. Store to ripen for at least three weeks and frost if desired.

Wacky Cake

Makes 8-in. cake

Dear Norma/

My mother tells me that back in the 1940s she had a cake recipe that was much like today's Snacking cakes. You mixed it right in the cake pan and it was called Wacky Cake. I don't use packaged foods, but sometimes long for the convenience they offer.

Is there any chance you might have this in your files?

Answer/

This is a great recipe to have on hand when you run out of eggs or milk.

1 1/2 cups all-purpose flour	1/2 cup vegetable oil
1 cup sugar	1 tbsp. vinegar
3 tbsp. unsweetened cocoa	1 tbsp. vanilla
1/4 tsp. salt	1 cup water
1 tsp. baking soda	

Sift into eight-inch square cake pan flour, sugar, cocoa, salt and baking soda. Measure oil, vinegar and vanilla into a measuring cup. Pour over flour mixture. Then pour on water, beating with a spoon until smooth. Even off batter and bake in 350F oven for 25 minutes or until cake tests done.

Rhubarb-date Cupcakes

Dear Norma/

In one of your recent columns was a reader request for Rhubarb-date Cupcakes which was in The Spectator some 20 years ago. This recipe was in the newspaper in 1972. It was my own creation and won the recipe-of-the-week prize.

I looked the recipe up in my scrapbook and here it is.

E. P. B. Beamsville

Answer/

I'm convinced no recipe is every lost. It is just tucked between the pages of someone's cookbook or in a scrapbook. Thanks to all the readers who found this recipe for us.

1 cup finely diced rhubarb	1/2 cup brown sugar
1 cup chopped dates	1 egg
1 tsp. baking soda	1 tsp. vanilla
1 cup boiling water	1 3/4 cups all-purpose flour
1/2 cup Crisco, room temperature	1 tsp. ground cinnamon
1/2 cup granulated sugar	1/2 tsp. ground cloves
1/2 tsp. salt	1/2 tsp. ground nutmeg

Wipe rhubarb with damp cloth and dice finely. Cut dates into not-too-large pieces. (Keep dates in plastic bag in cupboard, not refrigerator, for easier cutting). Mix rhubarb, dates and baking soda in bowl and stir in boiling water. Let cool to lukewarm.

In large bowl, cream Crisco, white and brown sugar together. Add unbeaten egg and vanilla and beat with spoon until fluffy. Sift flour, salt and spices over this mixture. Then pour lukewarm fruit over this mixture. Stir until flour is mixed in and beat until smooth.

Fill greased muffin cups, or line them with paper baking cups until they are three-quarters full. Bake at 350F for 20-25 minutes. Cool on wire rack. When cool, ice with butter icing. Can be served warm with ice cream. Freezes well.

Pies & Tarts

French Apple Pie

Dear Norma/

I'm looking for something completely different in an apple pie I could make ahead of time and freeze, unbaked. I'm having a guest in a few week's time and trying to prepare some desserts ahead of time.

Answer/

I've always said a fancy dessert in the freezer is like money in the bank. This French apple pie is different and after you try it you may never go back to the standard version.

Double crust pastry	**1/4 cup granulated sugar**
3/4 lb. apples, pared, cored and thinly sliced	**1/2 cup firmly-packed brown sugar**
2 tbsp. lemon juice	**2 tbsp. flour**
1/4 cup seedless raisins	**2 tbsp. butter**
3/4 tsp. cinnamon	**1/4 cup chopped toasted pecans**
1/4 tsp. nutmeg	**Brandy hard sauce**

Prepare pastry; line a nine-inch pie plate with half the pastry. Fill with apples and sprinkle with lemon juice and raisins. Combine cinnamon, nutmeg and granulated sugar in small bowl. Sprinkle over the apples. Blend brown sugar, flour and butter in small bowl until crumbs form. Mix in pecans. Sprinkle over filling. Roll remaining pastry for top. Cover pie; crimp edges to seal. To freeze: Wrap, label and freeze. It is best to use a rigid pie box so pastry edge will not be broken. Maximum recommended storage time: four months. To serve: Cut steam vents in top crust. Bake frozen pie at 450F for 10 minutes. Lower heat to 350F and bake another 40 minutes. If edge or top crust is browning too rapidly, cover with foil.

Brandy Hard Sauce

1/2 cup butter, softened	**1 tbsp. boiling water**
1 1/2 cups sifted icing sugar	**1 tsp. brandy**

Beat butter and sugar; add boiling water. Beat in brandy and serve the sauce with the pie. Serve the pie warm on warmed plates so the sauce melts down into the rich pie.

Deep Dish Apple Pie

Dear Norma/

My father, who lives with us, loves apple pie but has been told to cut down on the fat in his diet. If I could make a deep dish apple pie it would eliminate half the pastry, but I'm not quite sure how to go about this.

Answer/

I like Northern Spy apples in this type of pie, but you could use any type of cooking apples.

Pastry for single crust pie	**3 tbsp. flour**
9 cups sliced, peeled, cored	**1/2 tsp. salt**
cooking apples	**1/4 tsp. cinnamon**
1/2 cup white sugar	**1 tbsp. lemon juice**
1 cup packed brown sugar	**1 tbsp. butter (optional)**

Mix apples with sugars and flour and salt. Stir in lemon juice and place in buttered shallow two-quart baking dish. Dot with butter if desired and sprinkle with cinnamon. Roll out pastry to fit top of dish. Adjust and flute edges. With pastry brush, brush with a little milk and sprinkle lightly with sugar. Cut a few slits here and there to let steam escape. Bake in 425F oven 40 to 50 minutes until apples are tender and crust is nicely browned. Serve plain for low-fat diet. Or serve with one of the following: custard sauce, ice cream, whipped cream or Cheddar cheese.

Apricot Cream Pie

Dear Norma/

I see recipes for all kinds of fruit pies, but never one using apricots. Since this is my favorite fruit, I would like to be able to make a nice apricot cream pie with your help.

Answer/

This pie has a delicate apricot flavor and the swirled white and chocolate whipped cream topping makes it very festive indeed.

Baked pie shell	2 tbsp. butter
1/2 lb. dried apricots	2 tbsp. icing sugar
1/2 cup sugar	1/2 tsp. vanilla
4 tbsp. flour	1 cup whipping cream
1/4 tsp. salt	1/2 square unsweetened or
3/4 cup milk	semi-sweetened chocolate
2 egg yolks	

Wash apricots, drain and soak in cold water just to cover for 30 minutes. Cook until tender, then press through a wire sieve to make 1 1/4 cups pulp. Mix sugar, flour and salt together. Add milk, beaten egg yolks and apricot pulp. Cook over hot water (in double boiler) for 20 minutes, stirring frequently. Add butter, cool, pour into pie shell and chill. Whip cream and fold in icing sugar and vanilla. Spread two thirds of cream over pie. Melt chocolate over hot water; add to remaining whipped cream and swirl this onto the pie.

Mother Lucille's Pumpkin Pies   *Makes 2*

Dear Norma/

My pumpkin pies don't suit me at all. They are bright orange and don't have the good, spicy taste I remember from my grandmother's pies. I would be happy to have your own recipe for this type of pie.

Answer/

I'll do better than that. Here is my mother's recipe for making two, deep, richly-brown, spicy pies. They are so good that dinner leftovers are often eaten for breakfast by Megan and Michael, my grandchildren. The recipe, which is at least 65 years old, makes two 9-inch pies.

3 cups cooked (canned)
  pumpkin
2 cups brown sugar, packed
1 rounded tsp. ground ginger
2 heaping tsp. cinnamon
1/4 tsp. ground cloves
1/4 tsp. salt

4 cups whole milk (I use a can
  of evaporated milk plus
  enough milk to make the four
  cups)
6 eggs
2 pie shells

Mix sugar and spices. Beat eggs lightly. Add to sugar. Stir in pumpkin. Mix well. Add milk and combine. Have two nine-inch deep pie plates lined with your favorite pastry. Make sure filling is well stirred and divide between shells. Bake in preheated 450F oven for 20 minutes. Lower heat to 350F and continue baking for 25 minutes until crust is browned and filling is firm. Serve cold with sweetened vanilla-flavored whipped cream.

Marianne's Super Ice Cream Pie

Dear Norma/

Looking forward to the hot weather when nobody wants to bake, could we have a few frozen desserts to stash in the freezer?

Answer/

The easiest freezer dessert I make and keep in the freezer for unexpected guests is freezer ice cream pie. By varying the kind of ice cream and toppings, you can have a wide variety of pies. This came from a luncheon at East Plains United Church, Burlington.

Crust

1/3 cup smooth peanut butter   **1 cup Rice Krispies**
1/3 cup corn syrup

Mix together and press evenly into eight-inch foil pie pan.

Filling

Pile slightly softened ice cream into crust and freeze until required (wrapped in foil). Top with your favorite fruit sauce, blueberry, raspberry, pineapple, strawberry, or fudge sauce and toasted pecans.

Sometimes I drizzle the pie with butterscotch or chocolate sauce before freezing and slather it with toasted almonds. If you put the topping on before freezing, freeze the pie before wrapping.

Vary the kinds of ice cream as well. Mint ice cream is super with chocolate topping.

Cranberry Chiffon Pie

Dear Norma/

I want a light dessert to serve for Christmas dinner and was thinking of a cranberry chiffon pie. I have looked high and low through all my cookbooks but can't find such a recipe. Can you help me?

Answer/

When I was growing up in Moose Jaw, Sask., all we used cranberries for was sauce for turkey. Now we make muffins, pies, tarts, quick breads, molded salads, cookies and cobblers from the berries.

2 1/2 cups raw cranberries	3 stiffly beaten egg whites
1/2 to 3/4 cup water	1/2 cup sugar
3 egg yolks, beaten	2 tbsp. lemon juice
1/2 cup sugar	Pinch salt
1 envelope (1 tbsp.) gelatin	Baked pie shell

Cook cranberries in water until very soft. Put through a sieve. Add beaten egg yolks and the first half cup of sugar, which have been beaten together. Put in top of double boiler and cook 10 minutes, or until thickened, over hot water. Add gelatin which has been soaked in two tablespoons cold water. Cool.

When it has begun to set, fold in stiffly beaten egg whites which have been beaten with second half cup of sugar. Add lemon juice and salt. Pour into prepared baked crust. Chill several hours or overnight. Garnish with whipped cream and slivers of red and green maraschino cherries and some toasted, slivered almonds.

Eastern Townships Sugar Pie

Dear Norma/

I am wondering if you have a recipe for a delectable French-Canadian dessert called Sugar Pie? It is a very rich, sweet dessert and our whole family fell in love with it on a recent visit to Quebec. I would love to be able to make it at home.

Answer/

I'm going to give you two versions of this pie. The one from the Eastern Townships of Quebec is very simple to make. It is a perfectly smooth, fuller pie than the traditional sugar pie which has a thinner filling consistency, and the depth of filling is much less than for pies in general.

9-inch unbaked pie shell (do not prick)
1 1/2 cups corn syrup
1 cup sweetened, condensed milk
1/2 cup pecan halves

Combine corn syrup and condensed (not evaporated) milk on top of double boiler. Heat over boiling water for five minutes or until blended. Pour into prepared pie shell. Sprinkle with pecans. Bake in preheated 425F oven 10 minutes. Reduce heat to 350F and bake 20-25 minutes more, or until filling bubbles in centre.

Quebec Sugar Pie

9-inch pie shell, unbaked (do not prick)
2 cups lightly packed brown sugar OR 2 cups soft maple sugar, chopped
1 cup whipping cream
1/2 cup chopped nuts

Over low heat, bring brown sugar and cream or maple sugar and cream to a boil. Cook, slowly, stirring constantly, for 10 minutes or until thickened. Remove from heat and stir in nuts. Cool. Pour into prepared pie shell. Bake in preheated 375F oven 30-35 minutes. Cool. Filling will set when cold.

Old-fashioned Raisin Pie

Dear Norma/

Could you please print a recipe for old-fashioned raisin pie like my grandmother used to make? It was a juicy pie. When you cut a slice, the raisins and juice oozed out, not dry or jellied.

Answer/

Some raisin pies contain an egg and this creates the jellied-type filling. Raisin pie should always be served warm, especially if you want it runny and juicy. It can be made ahead and reheated.

2 cups seedless raisins, washed	1 tbsp. lemon rind, grated
2 cups boiling water	3 tbsp. lemon juice
1/2 to 1 cup brown sugar	Pastry for two-crust nine-inch
3 tbsp. all-purpose flour	pie

Place raisins and water in saucepan and cook until raisins are plump. Blend sugar with flour and add to raisin mixture and cook over low heat until thickened, stirring frequently. Add lemon rind, juice and pinch of salt. Stir. Cool. Line deep nine-inch pie plate with pastry. Pour in filling. Add top crust and seal. Make air vents. Pre-heat oven to 425F. Bake 40-50 minutes until nicely browned. Serve warm.

Vinegar Pie

Dear Norma/

I would like a recipe for vinegar pie. I saw it on a TV cooking show, but didn't get the directions.

Answer/

Pioneers said when there was no buttermilk and no maple syrup, or maple sugar, they could always whip up a vinegar pie.

1 1/2 tbsp. flour	2 egg yolks
1 cup sugar	1/4 cup milk
2 tbsp. vinegar	1 cup boiling water
1/2 tsp. salt	1 tsp. lemon extract
1 tbsp. butter	Baked pie shell

Mix flour and sugar. Add vinegar, salt, butter and beaten egg yolks. Beat together until creamy. Add milk and water and cook together in top of double boiler over hot water, stirring until mixture thickens. Flavor with lemon extract. Pour into baked pie shell and cover with meringue made with two beaten egg whites and four tablespoons sugar. Place in moderate oven until meringue is lightly browned.

Fresh Strawberry Tarts   *Serves 6*

Dear Norma/

I'm looking for a recipe for glazing fresh strawberry pie or tarts. I don't like the packaged glaze from the supermarket.

Answer/

Strawberries in season, plump, juicy and crimson are such a work of art that they deserve the best treatment possible. Try this way with fresh berry tarts.

2 pints fresh ripe strawberries, washed and hulled	**1 tbsp. cornstarch**
1/2 cup sugar	**1 tbsp. lemon juice**
	6 tart shells, large

Measure one heaping cup berries into a saucepan; place rest of berries in a bowl. Crush saucepan berries with a potato masher or wooden spoon. Add sugar, cornstarch and lemon juice and mix well. Cook over low heat, stirring constantly until mixture is clear.

Remove from heat and put mixture through a sieve. Let this glaze cool, then spoon it over strawberries in bowl.

Using a rubber scraper, carefully turn berries several times until they are all glazed. Heap glazed berries into tart shells, dividing fruit among them evenly.

Turn top berries pointed side up and spoon any remaining glaze over them. Serve at once, either plain or topped with whipped cream.

Lemon Butter Tarts   *Makes 15*

Dear Norma/

Some 25 years ago I was given a recipe for lemon butter tarts that became a favorite in our family. Now, the dear neighbor who gave it to me is deceased, and I cannot recall the exact ingredients. Can you please help?

Answer/

I'm sure you will understand that I couldn't possibly provide a recipe I have never seen. But I do think if you take a good butter tart recipe and add lemon juice, it might be similar to the one you have lost.

Prepare pastry for 15 medium-sized muffin cups. Do not prick.	**1/2 cup lightly-packed brown sugar**
Pre-heat oven to 375F.	**1 cup corn syrup**
1/2 cup raisins	**2 lightly-beaten eggs**
1/4 cup soft butter	**1 tsp. vanilla**
	4 tsp. lemon juice

Wash raisins and pour half cup boiling water over them in bowl. Let stand five minutes and drain. Stir together butter and brown sugar. Blend in corn syrup, eggs and flavorings. To prevent butter tarts from bubbling over, stir filling as little as possible. Stir in drained raisins. Fill pastry-lined muffin cups 2/3 full. Bake at 475F 15 to 20 minutes or until pastry is golden brown. Do not allow filling to bubble or hot syrup will seal tarts to edges of muffin cups and make tarts very hard to remove.

Cookies

Joanne's Best-ever Chocolate Chip Cookies

Dear Norma/

I collect chocolate chip cookie recipes and have several really good ones. Would you please send me your own favorite to add to my collection?

Answer/

When I made my favorite recipe for my two pre-school grandchildren, they gobbled them up and then told me "They weren't as good as Auntie Joanne's". I tracked down Joanne's recipe and here it is for your file.

1 cup granulated sugar
1 cup shortening (not butter or
  margarine)
1/2 cup brown sugar, packed
2 eggs
2 tsp. vanilla

2 cups all-purpose flour
1 tsp. baking soda
1 tsp. salt
1 12-oz. package (or two cups)
  jumbo chocolate chips

Cream shortening with sugar, egg and vanilla until light and fluffy. Add flour, baking soda and salt, sifted together. Blend well. Stir in chocolate chips (regular are all right but jumbo are better). Drop by teaspoonful onto lightly greased cookie sheets and bake 8 to 10 minutes or until golden brown in 375F oven. Remove to wire racks to cool and store in tightly covered tins.

Hint: If you are using coated, non-stick cookie sheets, lower heat to 350F and watch carefully. Cookies tend to burn easily on these new-type cookie sheets.

Unbaked Cookies

Dear Norma/

I don't like to heat up the kitchen with baking in the very hot weather but my kids love cookies. Do you have a recipe for cookies that don't need baking?

Answer/

Since this request comes every summer, here are three no-bake recipes for cookies the children should enjoy.

Marjorie's Unbaked Cookies

1/2 cup milk	6 level tbsp. cocoa powder
1/2 cup butter	3 cups rolled oats (not instant)
2 cups sugar	1 cup coconut

Blend milk, butter, sugar, and cocoa together in a saucepan and bring to a boil. Stir in the rolled oats and coconut. Form into small balls and place on lightly buttered cookie sheet and let stand until firm. Makes lots.

Frying Pan Cookies

2 unbeaten eggs	Pinch salt
1 cup sugar	2 cups Rice Krispies
1/2 cup washed dates, cut in pieces	Coconut

Put eggs, sugar, dates and salt in cold frying pan. Cook over low heat, stirring constantly 10 minutes. Remove from heat and add cereal. Using teaspoon, scoop out mixture, roll into balls and roll each in coconut. Cool and store in tins.

Peanut Butter Balls

1 cup icing sugar	1/2 cup chopped nuts
1 cup peanut butter	(walnuts, pecans or peanuts)
	1/2 cup chopped dates

Mix together, form into small balls, dip each into thin icing made from icing sugar mixed with milk until it is like heavy cream. Roll balls in desiccated coconut or finely chopped nuts. Store in tins after chilling.

Thimble Cookies

Makes 3 to 4 dozen

Dear Norma/

You never see thumbprint cookies at teas and receptions anymore. They were my favorite and I'd like to try them again if you can supply the recipe. The thumbprint was filled with red currant jelly.

Answer/

They were also called thimble cookies and dimple cookies. I'm sure I've made hundreds of them, but you are right. I haven't seen them for ages.

1/2 cup butter	1 slightly beaten egg white
1/3 cup sugar	1 cup finely-chopped walnuts
1 egg yolk	or pecans
1/2 tsp. almond flavoring	Red currant jelly
1 cup all-purpose flour	

Preheat oven to 325F. Lightly grease a cookie sheet. Cream butter and sugar together. Blend in egg yolk and almond flavoring. Stir in flour. Chill dough.

Shape into small balls. Dip each in beaten egg white and roll in chopped nuts. Place about one inch apart on prepared baking sheet.

Make a depression in centre of each with a thimble or your thumb. Bake in 325F oven for five minutes. Remove from oven and deepen depression. Bake another 8 to 10 minutes or until set.

Cool and fill depressions with red currant jelly.

Giant Cookies   *Makes 18*

Dear Norma/

We have three teenaged sons and my problem is trying to fill them up. Especially cookies. They come in and each takes a handful and in no time the cookie tins are empty again. I remember you writing that you had a big family of boys yourself. How did you cope?

Answer/

It wasn't easy! But I did learn not to make anything dainty and to double the recipe everytime I made cookies. Here is one for giant cookies that are chewy and really good. Double the batch.

2 medium bananas, peeled	2 eggs
2 cups granola (any kind)	1/2 cup margarine, melted
1 1/2 cups all-purpose flour	1/4 cup vegetable oil
1 cup packed brown sugar	1 cup chocolate chips (no need
1 tsp. ground cinnamon	to double this when doubling
1 tsp. baking powder	the recipe)

Slice bananas into blender. Whir until pureed. Combine granola, flour, sugar, cinnamon and baking powder until mixed. Stir in bananas, eggs, margarine and oil. Fold in chocolate chips.

To make cookies: spoon batter into quarter cup measure. Drop onto greased cookie sheets leaving room enough for big cookies to spread. Spread the batter to three-inch cookies. Bake at 350F for 17 minutes. Cool on wire racks.

Lumberjack Cookies

Dear Norma/

My mom used to make lumberjack cookies but when we moved she lost lots of her recipes. They had crinkly tops. Have you ever made lumberjack cookies? I sure hope so and you will put the recipe in the newspaper.

Answer/

You write a good letter for a 12-year-old boy. You can make either small cookies or ones as big as saucers.

2 cups sifted all-purpose flour	1/2 cup margarine
1/2 tsp. baking soda	1/2 cup sugar
1/2 tsp. salt	1/2 cup dark molasses
1 tsp ground cinnamon	1 egg
1/2 tsp. ground ginger	Sugar

Sift together flour, baking soda, salt, cinnamon and ginger and set aside. Beat room-temperature margarine until softened. Add half cup sugar gradually, creaming until fluffy. Blend in molasses. Add egg and beat thoroughly. Blending well after each addition, add dry ingredients in fourths to creamed mixture.

Chill dough thoroughly.

Form dough into balls using about two teaspoons dough for each (for teenagers, use four teaspoons for each ball of dough). Put some granulated sugar in a cereal bowl and roll each ball of dough in sugar. This gives the crinkly top. Put dough ball on greased cookie sheets. Bake at 350F about 10 minutes. Cool cookies on wire racks and store in covered tins. Makes about four dozen ordinary size cookies or two dozen biggies.

Fruit 'n' Fibre Cookies   *Makes 4 dozen*

Dear Norma/
I have some leftover oat bran and wonder if I could use it in some healthy-type cookies for my children's school lunches.
Answer/
These nutritious fruit and fibre cookies will use up one cup of your oat bran and fill a big cookie jar.

1 cup butter or margarine, softened
1/2 cup light brown sugar, packed
1 egg
2 tbsp. milk
1/2 tsp. vanilla
1 cup oat bran
1/2 cup all-purpose flour

1/2 tsp. baking soda
3 cups granola
1/2 cup pitted prunes, chopped and packed
1/2 cup dried apricots, chopped
1/2 cup walnuts or pecans, chopped

Preheat oven to 375F. Lightly grease two large cookie sheets. Beat butter and brown sugar with electric hand mixer at high speed until light and fluffy. Add egg, milk and vanilla and beat until well mixed.

In another bowl, combine oat bran, flour and baking soda and toss well. Add to butter-sugar mixture and beat at a low speed until blended. Stir in granola with wooden spoon. Mixture will be coarse and crumbly. Stir in fruit and nuts.

Scoop up the dough by generous tablespoons, form into one-inch balls and flatten slightly into discs. Place about one inch apart on prepared baking sheets.

Bake on middle rack of oven 12 to 14 minutes until golden brown. Cool on wire rack.

No-nut Crunchie Cookies

Dear Norma/

None of my children will eat nuts, not even peanuts, so a lot of cookie recipes are ruled out. Could you give me a recipe that four, six and eight-year-olds could help make and enjoy?

Answer/

The children could help measure and mix the dough and also roll it into balls and press the cookies down on the cookie sheet with a fork, but an adult had better handle the cooking chores.

1 cup cooking oil	1 tsp. vanilla
1 cup butter or margarine, room temperature	1/2 tsp. salt
	1 tsp. baking soda
1 cup dark brown sugar, packed	1 tsp. cream of tartar
	1 cup Rice Krispies
1 cup white sugar	1 cup regular oatmeal
1 egg	1 cup coconut
3 1/2 cups all-purpose flour	

Mix oil, butter, brown and white sugar together. Beat in egg and vanilla. Mix flour with baking soda, salt and cream of tartar. Stir into oil-sugar mixture. Stir in cereal, oats and coconut. Chill for 15 minutes.

Roll into balls and press down on greased baking sheet with a fork. Bake at 350F 10-12 minutes. Remove to wire racks to cool. Store in covered tins.

Cheesecake Bars

Dear Norma/

I love to serve cheesecake but so many of my friends are dieting and will only eat a sliver. Could I make cheesecake bars that would give smaller servings then the regular springform pan cheesecake?

Answer/

With calorie-counting friends, it is always a gracious touch to provide some fresh fruit and cheese as an alternative to the rich dessert you have prepared. For those who would prefer a small portion, these cheesecake bars should fill the bill.

5 tbsp. butter	1 (8-oz.) package softened
1/3 cup brown sugar	cream cheese
1 cup sifted all-purpose flour	1 egg
1/4 cup finely chopped walnuts	2 tbsp. milk
1/2 cup sugar	1 tbsp. lemon juice
	1/2 tsp vanilla

Preheat oven to 350F. In mixing bowl, cream butter and brown sugar. Add flour and finely chopped nuts. Mix well. Set aside one cup of this mixture for topping. Press remainder in bottom of lightly greased 8x8x2-inch cake pan. Bake 12 to 15 minutes.

Blend sugar and cream cheese until smooth. Add egg, milk, vanilla and lemon juice. Beat well. Spread over bottom crust. Sprinkle with reserved topping. Return to oven and bake 25 minutes longer. Allow to cool, then chill. Cut into bars.

Chocolate Peppermint Balls

Dear Norma/

I have a boy friend who is crazy about peppermint patties. I am hoping you can come up with a cookie that combines a chocolate cookie with a mint filling because I think it would blow his mind.

Answer/

When my children were growing up, their favorite Christmas cookies were chocolate peppermint balls. I hope your friend flips over them.

1/2 cup margarine	1 tsp. baking powder
2 cups brown sugar	1/2 tsp. salt
2 eggs	1/2 cup unsweetened cocoa
2 1/2 cups pastry flour	1 tsp. vanilla

Cream margarine and brown sugar. Add eggs, one at a time and beat. Sift dry ingredients and add to creamed mixture. Stir in vanilla. Chill dough two hours (must). Make into walnut size balls. Bake on greased cookie sheet in 350F oven for 12 to 15 minutes. They will flatten on bottom but be rounded on top. Put two cooled cookies together with peppermint icing to form round balls.

Peppermint Icing

1 1/2 cups icing sugar	2 drops oil of peppermint
2 tbsp. soft butter	Drop or two of green coloring
2 dessert spoons cream	(optional)

Mix all ingredients together and if necessary add a bit more sugar to make icing firm enough for filling. Store in covered tins.

Peanut Stuff

Dear Norma/

I would love to have a recipe that is a variation on the old standby Rice Krispie squares. Preferably one without marshmallows. My children will be so grateful.

Answer/

This peanut stuff is a favorite with children of all ages. You can vary the recipe by using Special K and pecans, or even mixed nuts if you chop them.

1 cup brown sugar, packed	1 cup peanuts
1 cup corn syrup	7 cups Rice Krispies or
1 cup peanut butter, smooth or	Corn Flakes
crunchy	

In large pot combine syrup, sugar and peanut butter. Cook, stirring for five minutes. Remove from heat and, working quickly, stir in peanuts and cereal. Turn into buttered 9x13x2 inch pan. Press down with moist glass bottom. Cool and cut into squares.

Orange Squares

Dear Norma/
One of my children is allergic to both chocolate and nuts. I would appreciate a recipe for some kind of squares she could enjoy.

Answer/
Orange and raisin flavors combine in this pan of squares to tempt both children's and adults' appetites. If you like, ice them with a thin glaze made from icing sugar moistened with orange juice.

1/2 cup shortening	1 tsp. baking soda
1 cup sugar	1 tsp. baking powder
1 egg	1/2 tsp. salt
Juice and grated rind of one	1 cup sour milk
large orange	1 cup raisins, washed and
2 cups flour	drained

Cream together shortening and sugar. Add egg and orange juice and rind. Sift together flour, baking soda, baking powder and salt and add to creamed mixture alternately with sour milk, beginning and ending with flour additions. Stir in raisins.

Place in greased 9x14x2-inch pan and bake for 35 minutes in 350F oven. Let cool before cutting into squares.

Mississippi Mud Brownies

Dear Norma/

My brownies are always on the dry side and I'd like to try a new recipe. My family is lucky enough not to have any weight problems so I don't mind how rich the recipe is, just so long as the brownies are moist and tasty.

Answer/

Perhaps you are cooking your brownies too long. Try these Mississippi mud brownies topped with marshmallows and chocolate icing. Really gooey and rich.

1/2 lb. margarine	2 cups sugar
1/2 cup cocoa	1 1/2 cups flour
4 eggs slightly beaten with a	1 tsp. vanilla
pinch of salt	3/4 cup chopped walnuts

Melt margarine and cocoa in heavy pan. Remove from heat and stir in sugar and eggs. Mix well. Add flour, nuts and vanilla and mix well. Spoon into greased 9x13-inch cake pan and bake at 350F for 30-35 minutes. Test in centre with toothpick. It should be a little gooey. It may take as long as 45 minutes but do not bake until pick comes out dry.

Icing

3 1/2 cups icing sugar, packed	3/4 cup chopped nuts
1/2 cup milk	1/2 package miniature
1/3 cup cocoa	marshmallows
1/4 cup margarine	

Sift icing sugar and add rest of ingredients except marshmallows. If icing is too stiff to spread, add a few drops more milk. As soon as brownies come out of oven, cover with marshmallows so they'll melt a little. When cool, cover with icing and let icing set for about an hour before cutting.

Hello Dolly Squares

Dear Norma/

I know you have printed the recipe for Hello Dolly squares before in your column but could you please print it again? It has been my standby for years and I have misplaced it.

Answer/

This has to be the most frequently requested of all recipes. But you must remember that recipes have legs. They walk away. When you clip a recipe you want to save, paste it inside the cover of a cookbook or even inside a kitchen cabinet door.

1/4 cup butter	1 cup semi-sweet chocolate
1 cup graham wafer crumbs	chips
1 cup coconut	1 cup toasted walnut pieces
	1 can sweetened condensed milk

Melt the butter in a nine-inch square cake pan and mix in the graham wafer crumbs. Spread evenly over bottom of pan. On top of this spread the coconut, then the chocolate chips, then the nuts. Pour the sweetened condensed milk evenly over top. Bake in 350F oven for 30 minutes. Cool and cut into squares.

Note: For special occasions, I have iced these with a butter icing tinted pale pink or pale green, but only for friends with an especially sweet tooth.

Candy

Mom's Peanut Brittle

Dear Norma/

My children love peanut brittle as a treat but on my limited food budget, I find it too expensive to buy. Can it be made cheaper at home? And would I have to have a candy thermometer?

Answer/

For perfect results every time I really recommend you invest in a candy thermometer. It is less expensive than one unsuccessful batch of candy. I turn my brittle out onto a big slab of marble my son Paul bought me for Christmas for $5 when he was a teenager, but a buttered cookie sheet will do as well.

1 cup corn syrup	1 1/2 cups peanuts, either red-
1/8 tsp. salt	skin or white
1 cup sugar	2 tbsp. hot water
1/4 cup water	1 tsp. baking soda
2 tbsp. margarine	

Heavily butter a large cookie sheet. Use a heavy-bottomed pot (I use my pressure cooker without the top). Stir together syrup, salt, sugar, 1/4 cup water and margarine. Cook to soft-crack stage or 280F on a candy thermometer.

To test in cold water, half fill a one-cup measure and drip a spoonful into the water. It will separate into threads that are soft but not brittle.

Stir in the nuts gradually so mixture continues to boil. Cook, stirring frequently, to hard-crack stage, 300F on thermometer, or until threads tested in cold water are hard and brittle. Color of mixture darkens slightly. Remove from heat. Stir baking soda into hot water and stir well into brittle mixture. Turn out quickly onto prepared baking sheet and with well-buttered spatula spread as thin as possible. Cool slightly. Turn brittle upside down and stretch thin. Cool. Crack into pieces and store in tightly covered tin.

Do not make on a hot, humid day.

Microwave Two-minute Fudge

Dear Norma/

I have never had any luck making fudge. It always goes sugary or doesn't set. A friend told me you have a secret recipe for no-fail microwave fudge that turns out perfectly creamy every time. Could you possibly part with this recipe?

Answer/

There is no such thing as a secret recipe as far as I am concerned. I am always astonished by people who won't share their favorite recipes with friends. This recipe has appeared in Stoveline several times over the years and I am happy to share it once more. It originated at a food editors' conference at the Waldorf Astoria in New York City many years ago and I am sure I have made tons of it since that time.

1 tbsp. instant coffee granules	1/4 lb. butter or
2 tbsp. milk	block margarine
1/4 tsp. salt	3 1/2 cups icing sugar,
1 tbsp. vanilla	packed into cup

In microwave-safe mixing bowl, melt butter or margarine. Add milk, coffee granules, salt and vanilla. Stir in icing sugar until well mixed. Microwave on high for two minutes. Bottom of bowl should feel warm. Remove from microwave; stir in one cup toasted, chopped walnuts. Line a bread pan with double layer of waxed paper, letting ends of paper extend over end of pan for grasping. Spoon fudge into pan and refrigerate for one hour. Grasp waxed paper ends and lift fudge from pan. With sharp knife, cut into squares.

In warm weather, refrigerate.

Variation: Leave out the coffee granules and add 1/4 cup cocoa to icing sugar.

Cec's Almond Rocha

Dear Norma/

Would you have a recipe for Almond Rocha in your food files? I am looking for the type with a buttery-butterscotch type middle with dark chocolate coating on both sides.

Answer/

A cousin from Vancouver brought this recipe to our Muskoka cottage at Thanksgiving years ago and I have been thankful for it ever since. You must use butter - margarine doesn't work. I've tried it. The cooking is lengthy, but the wonderful candy is worth it.

1 cup granulated sugar	1/4 lb. slivered almonds,
1/2 lb. butter	toasted before you begin
1 tbsp. corn syrup	6 oz. Merkin's semi-sweet
3 tbsp. water	chocolate wafers

Put all ingredients except nuts and chocolate into heavy-bottomed pot. Over medium heat, stir until sugar is dissolved. Lower heat to medium-low and cook, stirring occasionally, to the hand-crack stage when tested in cold water, or 300F on a candy thermometer.

Spread almonds over 3/4 of a well-buttered cookie sheet. Pour hot candy quickly over almonds, spreading with buttered spatula. Cool. Melt chocolate over warm water. Ice one side of candy with half the melted chocolate. Chill. Turn over and ice other side with rest of chocolate. Don't worry if candy breaks when you turn it. Just ice the pieces.

When chocolate sets, break into pieces and store in covered tin.

Kelly's Skor Bars

Dear Norma/

Just before Christmas I wrote to Stoveline requesting a recipe which you found for me. I told you I was making imitation Skor Bars and Peanut Butter cups. These are copy-cat recipes, but they taste very close to the real thing and take no time to make up.

Answer/

I am always delighted when readers share their favorite recipes with me in return for one I have been able to provide for them.

1 cup butter	1 1/2 cups chocolate chips,
3/4 cup brown sugar, packed	semi-sweet or milk chocolate
1 sleeve salted crackers	

Line a cookie sheet with aluminum foil. Lay crackers on foil, salted side up. Melt butter and brown sugar and heat until sugar is dissolved. Pour over crackers and bake in 350F oven for 13 minutes. Immediately sprinkle chocolate chips on top. When soft, spread over crackers.

I prefer to melt the chocolate and then pour it over the crackers. Score bars with a knife while chocolate is still soft. Refrigerate 30 minutes. Peel off foil and break into bars.

Kelly's Peanut Butter Cups

2 cups smooth peanut butter	1 6-oz. package milk
4 tbsp. butter	chocolate chips

Mix one cup peanut butter, butter and chocolate chips together. Melt until smooth over low heat or use a double boiler. Reserve one cup peanut butter for filling. Coat small foil cups with the peanut butter and chocolate mixture, making sure you coat the sides as well. Let them harden a little. Spoon in some peanut butter and cover with chocolate mixture. Set aside to harden.

Cathy's Caramel Corn *Makes 16 cups*

Dear Norma/

Is it possible to make caramel corn at home?

My husband, who is pencil-slim and doesn't count calories, likes it better than plain popcorn or potato chips as a snack and I would love to surprise him with my own homemade variety if you can supply the know how.

Answer/

I thought my caramel corn was pretty good until one Christmas when my daughter-in-law brought hers to the family gathering and shared the recipe. It's perfect.

1 cup redskin peanuts	1/2 tsp. salt
1 cup pecan halves	1 tsp. vanilla
1 cup slivered almonds	12 cups popped corn, popped
1/2 cup butter	in air popper without oil
1/3 cup corn syrup	or butter.
1 cup brown sugar, packed	

Spread nuts in large roasting pan. Bake in 350F oven for 10 minutes. In heavy saucepan, melt butter; add corn syrup, sugar and salt. Bring to a boil, stirring until sugar is dissolved. Boil for two minutes. Remove from heat and add vanilla. Pour over roasted nuts and popped corn in roasting pan and stir until well mixed. Bake in 350F oven for 15 minutes, stirring every five minutes.

Turn out immediately onto buttered baking sheets. Cool. Store in covered tins.

Miscellaneous

Bruschetta

Dear Norma/

I want to try my hand at making bruschetta. I have enjoyed this in an Italian restaurant, but I am sure it is not a restaurant secret. Is it too difficult to make at home?

Answer/

No, it is quite simple and delicious. This recipe put out by Kraft using this company's House Salad Dressing makes 20 two-inch slices.

1 baguette, split lengthwise	1 green onion, sliced
1/3 cup Kraft House Italian dressing	1/2 cup grated Parmesan cheese
3 tomatoes, seeded and chopped	Dried basil to taste

Heat broiler. With cut side up, toast bread lightly under broiler. Combine dressing, tomatoes and onion. Spoon over toasted bread; sprinkle with cheese and basil. Broil two minutes or until heated through. Cut into two-inch slices and serve in a napkin-lined basket.

Dale's Hot German Mustard

Dear Norma/

Do you have a recipe for uncooked German-type mustard?

Answer/

One summer I paid about $4 for a jar of this mustard in a cottage country gift shop. When my brother visited us from his Haliburton cottage he laughed at me and said he made his own and it cost practically nothing.

1 heaping tbsp. dry mustard	2 full-rounded tbsp. brown sugar
1 full-rounded tbsp. flour	White vinegar

Mix dry ingredients well. Add white vinegar gradually until right consistency. It thickens as it stands. Make up as needed.

Mom's Shake and Bake Mix

Dear Norma/
  One of my New Year's resolutions is to use less packaged foods and more homemade. Do you have a substitute for the package coating mix you shake in a bag to coat chicken pieces or pork chops.

Answer/
  You can experiment with this recipe and change the seasonings to suit your taste.

1/2 cup all-purpose flour	1 1/4 tsp. salt
1 tsp. cornstarch	1 tsp. sugar
1 tsp. paprika	5 tsp. vegetable oil
1 1/2 tsp. each onion powder	1 3/4 tsp. poultry spice, or sage
and garlic powder	1 cup fine, dry breadcrumbs

  Mix together in bowl as you would pastry, with your fingertips. Keep in a plastic bag in the freezer. Use on chicken pieces, fish fillets, pork or veal. Dip portions of meat or fish in water, shake in mix and place on baking sheet lined with foil. Cook chicken and meat at 400F for 30 minutes or until done; fish just until it flakes. Return unused coating to freezer.

Almost Twinkies Filling

Dear Norma/
  My friend has a recipe for that creamy white filling or icing that commercial bakeries use in products like Twinkies. She won't part with her recipe and I hope you have something similar.

Answer/
  This takes a lot of beating, but it resembles Twinkie filling.

1/4 lb. margarine (uncolored if	1 cup granulated sugar
you can find it)	3/4 cup evaporated milk
1/2 cup Crisco	1 tsp. vanilla

  Put in deep bowl and beat with electric mixer for 8 to 10 minutes until fluffy and sugar no longer gritty. Put between layers of sponge cake.

Miracle Homemade Pam

Dear Norma/

My neighbor says you have a wonderful recipe for coating muffin pans so the muffins don't stick to the pans. I don't use those little paper liners.

Answer/

This is the best thing since sliced bread!

In one pint sealer, put one cup vegetable oil and one tablespoon liquid lecithin (buy it at a health food store). Mix well. Using a small pastry brush, coat muffin tins including edges. The muffins get a beautiful surface and fall out of tins after baking. Refrigerate remainder of the "Miracle Pam" and mix thoroughly each time before using.

Baker's Icing

Dear Norma/

Could you please print a recipe for that kind of whipped icing bakers use to ice cakes and make the kind of flowers and leaves that stay soft?

Answer/

Usually I don't try to duplicate commercial recipes but this one was given to me by a baker friend who said he doesn't mind if I give it to readers.

1/2 cup Crisco	Pinch salt
1/2 cup butter	1 tsp. clear vanilla (from cake
1/2 cup milk	decorating shop)
3/4 cup granulated sugar	7 tbsp. flour

Have all ingredients at room temperature and combine. Beat at high speed on electric mixer for five minutes.

This icing can be colored and used through icing tubes for flowers, leaves, etc. It does not get hard. This is enough for layer cake and sides.

Index